OCEAN OF CONSCIOUSNESS

The 756 Names, Qualities, and Attributes of Mirabai Devi

A Poetic Treatise Celebrating the Light of the Divine Feminine

Rama Pemmaraju Rao, MD

Edited by Sherwood Lee

Published by Harrison House | San Antonio, Texas

Ocean of Consciousness: The 756 Names, Qualities, and Attributes of Mirabai Devi
A Poetic Treatise Celebrating the Light of the Divine Feminine
Copyright © 2016 by Ramakrishna Pemmaraju Rao (originally penned March 2012). All Rights Reserved.

This book may not be reproduced, transmitted, or stored in whole or in part by any means, including graphic, electronic, or mechanical without the express written consent of the publisher except in the case of brief quotations embodied in critical articles and reviews. Any reproductions without written permission from the publisher are illegal and punishable by law. Please purchase only from authorized distributors to protect the author's rights.

PUBLISHER'S NOTE
The opinions expressed in this manuscript are solely the opinions of the author and do not represent the opinions or thoughts of the Publisher. The author has represented and warranted full ownership and/or legal right to publish all the materials in this book. The publisher does not have any control over and does not assume any responsibility for author or third party websites or their content.

Harrison House Publishing
www.theharrisonhousepublishing.com
info@theharrisonhousepublising.com

Harrison House Publishing and the "HH" logo are trademarks belonging to Harrison House Publishing.

For information contact:
Dr. Rama Pemmaraju Rao at Enlightened Medicine
http://www.drramaenlightenmentmd.com

Book and Cover design by Rama Pemmaraju Rao and Sherwood Lee
Front and back cover original art by Rama Pemmaraju Rao. Front cover: *Mirabai Immersed in Divine Light*. Back cover: *Mirabai Enthroned Upon the Altar of Eternity and Oneness*.

ISBN: 978-0-9061285-9-2

First Edition: April 2016

10 9 8 7 6 5 4 3 2

PRINTED IN THE UNITED STATES OF AMERICA

Library of Congress: 2016938895

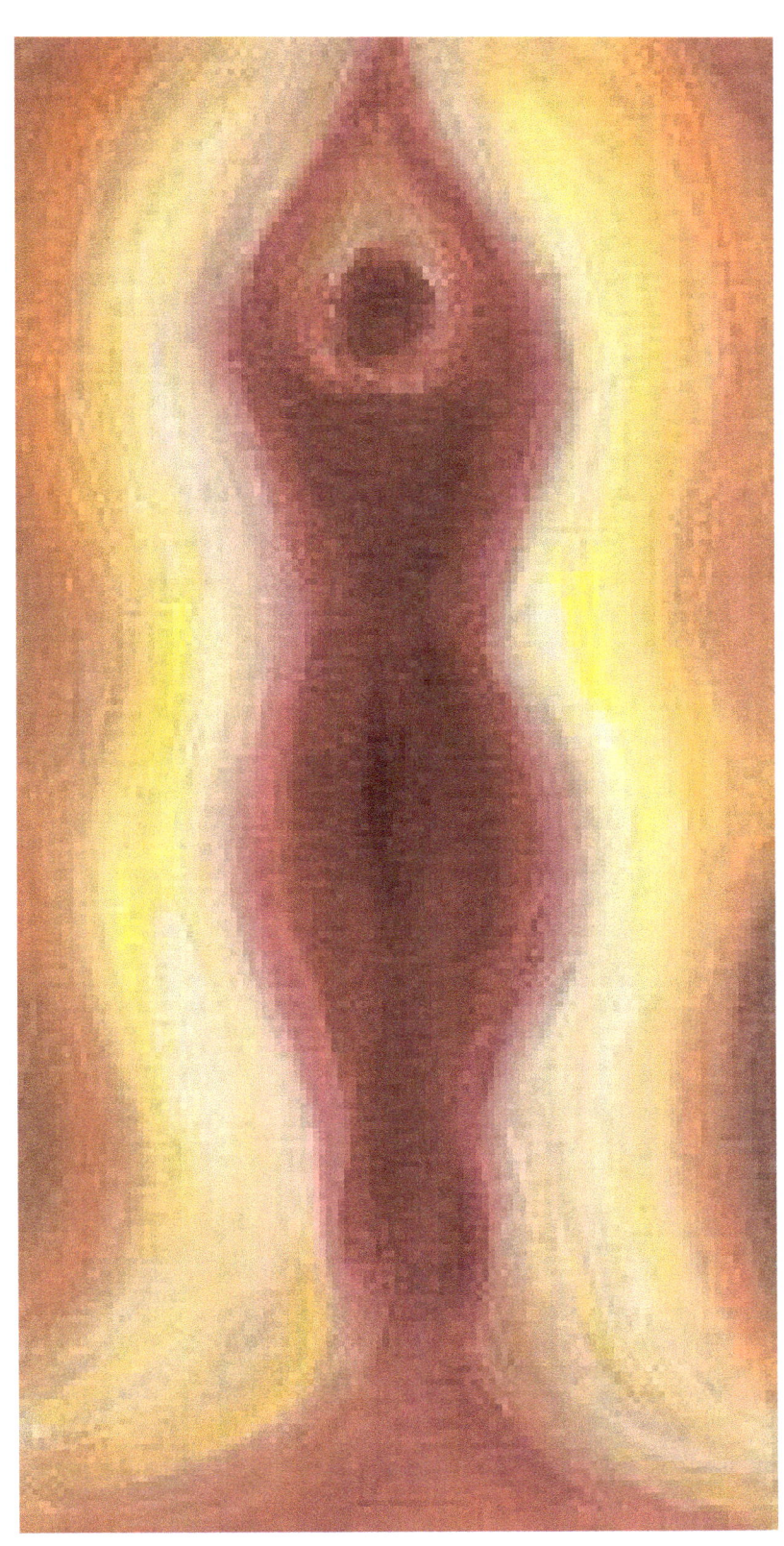

DISCLAIMER

Dr. Rama Pemmaraju Rao has sincerely and lovingly brought forward this book for the inspiration of all. These names, qualities, and attributes of Mirabai Devi are his original interpretation received in his meditations and from personal guidance. They are written only to uplift humanity and to represent poetically the loving description of the Higher Self qualities of Mirabai Devi.

This book is not a biography; rather, it is a poetic piece of literature written solely for the purpose of expounding the power of unconditional love, light, and inspiration that is possible. Beings like Mirabai, to the best of their ability, manifest these sacred qualities through their work, person lives, and service to humanity and Mother Earth. In essence, we all have these Higher Self qualities when our own bodies and minds are aligned with our own Higher Selves and Spirits.

A portion of proceeds from the sale of this book will go to the Mirabai Devi Foundation.

TABLE OF CONTENTS

DEDICATION 1

PREFACE 3

MOTHER QUOTATION (from the sayings of Rama) 9

INTRODUCTION 11

756 NAMES, QUALITIES, AND ATTRIBUTES 16

    Lines 1 – 108 16

    Lines 109 – 216 25

    Lines 217 – 324 34

    Lines 325 – 432 43

    Lines 433 – 540 52

    Lines 541 – 648 61

    Lines 649 – 756 70

GLOSSARY 79

DEDICATION

This book is lovingly and humbly dedicated to the Divine Source or Light, especially the cosmic feminine principle, who made this book possible. I am honored the names, attributes, and qualities of Mirabai Devi flowed through me and onto countless pages through sleepless nights to describe an infinitesimal fraction of the gifts, beauty, and divinity of Mirabai Devi.

I am also grateful her guides and guidance used me to create a wonderful new text for her birthday in March of 2012, and I believe this text was a Soul contract between Mirabai and myself ages ago upon this planet Earth. This book was created in the year of the new Golden Age, 2012, which marks the beginning of the next 10,200 years of extraordinary evolution of consciousness upon this planet Earth. How timely the Divine is in creating this text.

Although tailored to describe Mirabai's unique qualities, as well as journey in her present incarnation, I am filled with inspiration that each and every line of this book also applies to all of us, as well for the Cosmic Divine Mother, who flows through all and manifests through those who simply agree to remember that we too are indeed none other than the Divine Mother herself. In reading these lines suffused with cosmic light, love, and inspiration, individuals will awaken and unfold those divine qualities of the Divine Mother also within themselves, buried under the heap ashes of time, space, and long forgotten memories of their oneness in Spirit.

Rama Pemmaraju Rao, MD
March 2012-2016 (Four years later after composing these and on Mirabai's 46th birthday.)
This book was originally penned March 2012.

PEMMARAJU RAO

PREFACE

It was the fall of November 2007, when I first met Mirabai Devi. A lifelong student of enlightenment, I have always been drawn by inspiration to those divine souls who are uplifting humanity in large and small ways and especially those who carry their mission with the highest aspects of unconditional love. I first met her when I was going through an extraordinarily difficult period in my life, after I heard about her through an acquaintance. After seeing her, I immediately knew that we had been connected in many past lives—physical and non-physical. I knew I had to meet her right away and so I flew to Boston that Fall to meet her at a small retreat center nestled in the forest. When I first laid eyes on her, she was walking through the trees and into a little house to have her healing session with me. My first impression was that she was beautiful, light, and spritely. She reminded me of the Goddess Artemis, prancing and sauntering about the forest, blessing Nature as Nature blessed her. After I shared my woes with her in a little cabin set up for her sessions, she quickly clicked her fingers and brought forward Divine Light that surrounded me and charged the entire room. In that moment a new spark and ray of hope filled me from head to toe, beyond even what is body and mind. I experienced unconditional love in that moment suffused with healing in a timeless space, and knew that she had a divine role to play in my life and I in hers. Since that time, it has been a relationship in evolution and revolution.

Since childhood and over many lifetimes for that matter, I have had the burning desire to know and experience the Divine Mother principle, the element of unconditional love within the heart, and the pervading force throughout the Universe. I have been upon the journey of honoring and remembering her. She is the aspect of Source or Creator in the form of the Divine Feminine, the infinite Cosmic Mother responsible for the seen and unseen, and known and unknown worlds. It is through her will and action and through her power of infinite love that anything and everything is created, maintained, or destroyed.

Our earthly mother's love is the closest representation to that of the Divine Mother. What mother, no matter what difficulties or problems she faces and despite anything negative that her own child has done will not defend, love, and protect that child? The same is true of the plant and animal kingdom, as well. Nature itself is the Divine Mother. She is the mysterious power, the living force that animates creation, and the cycle of birth and death of all sentient and insentient beings. Nothing can happen ultimately without the Divine Mother's power. Scientists are on the brink of discovering that as they find smaller and smaller particles -- the root of the animation and creation of the minutest particles is that of love and divine light.

This love is personified as the Divine Mother in all cultures. The greatest mystery is that this love is unborn, undying, and always present and forms itself out of itself, out of the bosom of the Divine Original Source or Silent Creator. Out of silence, all of creation emerges, sustains, and finally dissolves. This great emanation, this supreme manifestation out of the vast silence of Source is the Divine Mother.

The Divine Mother energy is a deep and divine quagmire. The quintessential explanation, remembrance, and experience of the Divine Mother exists in all ancient cultures, seemingly forgotten by the modern world, but now re-awakening in the hearts and minds of mankind. The lore of India, especially, is impregnated with knowing and understanding her vast, infinite mysteries, principles, and beguiling ways. She is known in infinite millions of forms and is worshipped in countless ways. The basic principle is that she springs out of the Will of Silent Creator Source and yet, ironically, has the Supreme Will of her own even the original Creator must abide by.

Mother Kali, the incredibly ferocious aspect of the Divine Mother who springs out of the seemingly silent and the sleeping Shiva who lies on the ground in the Hindu depictions, best describes this principle. Even the primordial Shiva cannot stop the workings of Divine Kali once she is set in motion; he must relent to her awesome power that yet still comes out of Silence itself.

In this new era of the Divine Feminine there are many living teachers, masters, divine mothers, light workers, teachers, gurus, savants, sages, rishis, avatars, and any and all who are now remembering and imbibing the goddess energy in life and living.

Throughout the ages there have been those who have been able to harness and capture a portion of this infinite love and light and channel it through their own being. In fact, some merge into the energy and become the Divine Mother in living human form. This is known as enlightenment and identification with the Mother principle for those who resonate with the Divine Feminine. When enlightenment takes place, an individual merges with that which is nearest and dearest to his or her own heart. So, the great masters of yesteryear and yore and those of today sometimes choose to harness the power of the Mother for the benefit of humanity. Some even say that the energy of the Divine Mother herself comes down to the Earth Plane to take on a body for the benefit and uplifting of this planet and countless other worlds. India seems to be the reservoir of unconditional love and so many have chosen to come down into that culture for the benefit of all. With this energy anything and everything can happen to those around the Divine Mother and from a distance to those who tune into such beings. Beautiful inner cleansings, transformations, and insights begin to arise and our lives on the outside begin to improve and blossom in ways we could never dream possible. This is the spiritual journey that a Divine Mother or similar being initiates for us, the journey that leads back to our own hearts, to our own power and love so we may live life to the fullest and with the highest of qualities and with freedom from lower qualities that get in the way of our peace and prosperity. A Divine Mother presence on Earth is here for only one purpose: that of uplifting others in any and all ways mainly through the mysterious power of Grace -- the actual force of the Cosmic Mother herself that causes true change and transformation.

There are many Divine Mothers working in public and behind the scenes as they are helping to harness and capture the essence of the Divine Feminine and spread into all aspects of humanity. As generations come, there will be many more in line to take birth for spectacular and profound earthly missions, as this planet is now a haven of spiritual, emotional, mental, and physical evolution, unprecedented upon this beautiful Earth.

Since 1987, our planet has been graced by the "return of the goddess." What this means is that the silent Creator through his or her will has made an intention for the return to the remembrance of the softer side of life and living, to remember all aspects of unconditional love, mercy, compassion, grace, understanding, and the valuing and honoring of feelings and emotions. The intention to value the arts of all kinds and to uphold their importance is thus returning to the planet. This love is now being suffused into all careers and in all aspects of life and is affecting mass humanity. The ushering in of the Divine

Feminine in 1987 also set up the foundation for the new Golden Age that began in 2012 and will continue to evolve for the next 10,200 years. In this period, there are great progenitors who are holding the Divine Light for future generations with great care, confidence, and sacrifice.

Some predecessors have come as the Divine Mother, while others hold aspects of her for this purpose. Our world is transforming from overemphasis on mentally thinking things out in logical ways to allowing emotion and feeling to be our real guide. Harsh patriarchy that has claimed this planet is being replaced by love. This patriarchal way of relating through condition, judgment, harshness, logic, and everything left brained is being balanced by all right brain energy through the power of love and understanding. What amazing times we live in!

Mirabai is one such teacher and being. Hailing from South Africa, the gateway between East and West, she is a truly a gifted way-shower, guardian, protector, mentor, master, teacher, healer, and embodiment of the infinite Divine Mother. Through arduous spiritual practice from many of her past lives, she has been gifted with spontaneous enlightenment at a young age and has merged her individuality with the Divine Source. Taking this energy into her heart, she helps uplift humanity in large and small ways.

The Divine Light gifted these names of Mirabai through me. It was March of 2012, when I was guided to stay up continuously for almost three days composing the first 108 names. The rest of the 756 names came in spurts through endless sleepless nights as I was carried by the Divine Light without fatigue! There are actually more names to be channeled for the actual 12 chakras, but it is not determined as yet when and how those will come through.

These names are unique and describe her Higher Self, her mission, and her life. In India it is a tradition that when a Divine Mother descends or when an advanced being with some of the Mother's qualities comes down to Earth for a spiritual mission a new scripture may be born. Usually, the 108 names arise from an inspired person or group who brings down the qualities, attributes, and experiences of that particular teacher, mentor, guide, Divine Mother, or Guru. In this case, the inspiration blossomed into 756 names, 108 times seven for each of the sacred chakras or energy centers within the human form along the spinal column, which is the central core of the Light Body that carries the energy of enlightenment for any and all. Interestingly, usually, these 108 names are in direct Sanskrit and have to be painstakingly translated into English. In this case, they are in English and will be translated in future generations into Sanskrit.

These 756 attributes, which came through me, amaze even me. People cannot grasp the depth and breadth of their meaning in one reading; rather, they are forever imbibed with deep mystery and wonder. They are a gift to her from higher beings of light and love and to humanity. Reading them or repeating the lines invokes the sacred grace of devotion to the Divine, awakens the heart, and automatically creates a line of communication with Mirabai's Higher Self to an individual's Higher Self. In fact, there is nothing in these names that is not also in us, as we, too. are the Divine Mother, but in varying degrees of awareness of it, as we all are ultimately the Divine Mother, embodiments of unconditional love.

For those inspired to read these names, attributes, and qualities of Mirabai Devi and work to understand them, there are many blessings seen and unseen, known and unknown received for their own uplifting and evolution. May all seek and find the Divine Mother inside their hearts and throughout the entire Cosmos, for we are all the very essence of the Divine Feminine and the Sacred Masculine and yet, beyond both.

Rama Pemmaraju Rao, MD
Spring 2016

PEMMARAJU RAO

> Without a Mother, One Cannot Love.
> Without a Mother, One Cannot Die.
> -- ***Herman Hesse***

Dr. Rama Pemmaraju Rao goes onto say:

Without the Divine Mother, One cannot live
With the Divine Mother, only then can one truly die

With the Mother, only then can one truly live
With the Divine Mother, only then can one truly love

And further, from his sayings:

The essence of divinity is the Mother
The essence of Mother is divinity
The Mother of essence is divinity
The Mother of divinity is the ESSENCE

INTRODUCTION

Dallas, Texas
March 2012
For Her Auspicious Birthday during this historic
Millennial Shift in Consciousness upon the Planet Earth

Welcome to this most authentic poetic prose. It is truly a gift of grace from the Divine Light, to Mirabai upon her birthday in 2012, and to global humanity. It symbolizes her attributes, qualities, names, and experiences in a unique manner through 756 sacred lines of words. The first 756 names were literally channeled by me several days prior to her 2012 birthday and, subsequently, on many, many sleepless days and nights, the other lines effortlessly came to me. It is now Her birthday 2016, and four challenging but important years have gone by for me. I am now inspired to finish this book exactly at her birthday time . . . once again! Divine timing and Grace upon this day: March 12, 2016!

In India, it is traditional for rishis, devotees, friends, well-wishers, disciples, gurus, and others to compose an inspirational 108 names to a saint, spiritual teacher, guru, avatar or other spiritual beings as a gift to all. These 108 names describe the mission, qualities, attributes, and personality of one who descends from higher worlds to help global humanity. These 108 names are traditional because the number 108 is sacred, and the numbers that make up 108 added together equal the number 9, which reduces to 3. In this Universe "3" is a powerful number, reflecting the trinity and many other manifestations of 3. We often clap three times, ring bells three times, and so on. Nothing seems complete without often doing something a total of three times. Is it not so?

This subject of sacred numbers is vast, but suffice it to say the 108 names are often the tradition. This book, however, went to 756 names, which is 108 times 7, for each of our sacred inner chakras or centers of light deep within our bodies and beings experienced and discovered through spiritual practices. This book will one day go onto another 108 times 5 for the additional 5 chakras equaling a total of 12 chakras. Repeating, remembering, or reading these names interestingly, lovingly, and automatically take individuals to a space of Divine Light. These names also reflect who we are: images of the Divine Mother and any and all other aspects of the Divine Source.

In the teachings of enlightenment, the Divine Source is everywhere, in all things at once, and knows and feels all at once. It suffuses all, creates and sustains, and destroys all only to recycle everything again within its own bosom and being. No place exists without the Source and the Source came out of itself in an unending flow that has no beginning or end. We are an embodiment of Source, but some of us have temporarily forgotten this, caught within the limits of our bodies and minds through many incarnations in this physical world and many other physical and non-physical worlds.

Throughout the ages, many different higher beings from many worlds came to the Earth plane and other similar worlds on any and all levels to help reawaken global humanity to their Divine potential and remembrance. For those who listen and consciously practice this remembrance, their long forgotten enlightenment is ultimately revealed. This use of Divine remembrance is the greatest gift from such enlightened beings to us.

This kind of text is one form of spiritual manifestation and practice among many -- chanting, devotion of any kind, conscious creativity, meditation, self-inquiry and contemplation, selfless service, physical postures, and breath work – and all are designed to get us to wake up from the bonds of the mind and from limited thinking to understanding the vastness of consciousness that lies within us. As we know, only a fraction of our brainpower is used; the rest is a mystery.

It is my feeling this other part of brain and its energy and light, and so much more, is involved in a vast knowledge known as enlightenment. So, kindly enjoy this text and reflect on its meaning because each line, although tailored to the Nature of Mirabai, her personality, and Mission, can still apply to us for we also embody these Divine attributes.

Each line is deeply mysterious. Infused with cosmic light and wisdom, people can read it one way and come back to gather an even deeper and enriching meaning the next time. Reading or even chanting these lines will spontaneously take an individual into a state of oneness, light, peace, and bliss. Reading these in addition to other spiritual practices actually reverses the life force. Instead of always focusing on the outer world, we are spontaneously led by Divine Grace into a state of love and light that is beyond and behind and even within our own mind and bodies we normally are not aware of. By reading these lines particularly written for Mirabai by her own Divine guides through me, we are led to a sample of the type of light and bliss she experiences all the time.

Each Saint, Master, or Divine Mother comes here upon his or her unique ray of light. These rays are infinite. No two rays are alike, just as we are all unique. Similarly, we all also have our unique ray. We just have to awaken this light and trust it.

Mirabai is one who through many lives has discovered her own unique ray of light and now has the ability to offer this light to others to help transform, expand, heal, and uplift. When we sit in her midst we experience her unique wavelength, just as we would experience a different kind with another being like her on the planet, until we find our own and live in that state of oneness with our own soul consciously all the time. The intention of these 756 names, then, is to uplift humanity in large and small ways.

Mirabai Devi means the "boundless ocean of consciousness" through the auspices of the Divine Feminine Principle in Sanskrit. It also means the "one who bestows prosperity and abundance," as she is the power of abundance itself. By reciting these names and attributes of Mirabai Devi, which I was inspired by the Light to write down, we are uplifted and drawn into the state that she rests in all the time. We remember our own divinity by praising and acknowledging her, as she is a perfect mirror of our own state of pure enlightenment.

These 756 names, qualities, and attributes are written in English with the intention to translate them into Sanskrit at a later time. Quite the opposite task since most are written in Sanskrit while the West struggles to translate into English!

Each name, quality, or attribute in English ends with the chanting of "Om Aim Shreem Hreem Mira Devi Shakthyai Namaha," which means "Salutations to the boundless ocean of consciousness, the embodiment of Saraswati (wisdom, creativity, education, speech, medicine, elocution, art, architecture, science, and intelligence), Lakshmi (prosperity, wealth, and abundance), and Durga (the cosmic power of the Divine Mother)." Aim, Shreem, and Hreem are powerful bija mantras or seed letters that awaken these attributes that lay dormant or partially awake within us all yet, fully awakened within an enlightened Avatar like Mirabai. The word Sri not only means title of respect, but also means the energy of prosperity and fullness.

In Sanskrit, Saraswati means "she who has flow," that is, the never ending flow of knowledge, wisdom, creativity, expression, and the arts. Lakshmi derives from the root Lakshya, which means "aim or goal the primordial force of infinite abundance," while Durga means "fort, difficult to overrun, and the one who eliminates sufferings."

Chanting or reciting these words even in English with purity and sincerity draws the instantaneous grace, protection, guidance, support, and love of Mirabai Devi along with the Light of Para Atman (The Supreme Light) as Mirabai is merged with the Light of Para Atman.

When translated into Sanskrit later, each name will start with "OM" (the primordial sound) and end in "Namaha" (salutations to).

However, for initial purposes here and to get started in this book, each name and attribute on each line begins with "Salutations to Mirabai Devi, who…" and then at the end of each attribute "Aum Aim Shreem Hreem Mira Devi Shakthyai Namaha" can be chanted within if an individual wants to do so.

756 NAMES, QUALITIES, AND ATTRIBUTES OF SRI MIRABAI DEVI

1 – 108

Salutations to Sri Mirabai Devi:

1. whose name means the "boundless ocean of consciousness"

2. who is the Supreme Goddess and the Healing Feminine and who has assumed a body and descended from the Supreme Light to heal and enlighten mankind

3. who is Tripura Sundari, the triad of Saraswati, Lakshmi, and Durga

4. who is Ishwari, the sovereign queen and the Divine consort of Ishwara, the Supreme Deity of Light

5. whose own Sankalpa or will guided her to be born in the land of South Africa to represent the golden bridge between East and West

6. who arrived to assist and heal Bhoomi Devi, Mother Earth, and to help her ascend

7. who is a Bodhi Sattva, who also postponed the enjoyment of Heaven for the sake of the suffering, like her beloved sister Quan Yin

8. who is the embodiment of the Goddess Kundalini Shakti, whose brilliance shines like countless crimson and vermillion bolts of lightening, golden and silver like the rising moon, and copper rose from the setting sun

9. who is clad in white and gold garments and a shimmering jeweled tiara, representing the pure effulgent Light of Para Atman

10. whose angelic, bewitching smile captivates the righteous, as well as the most wicked of the wicked, and whose melodious voice beckons the devotee, as well as the ogre to drown in her vast Ocean of Bliss

11. whose most beautiful eyes, complexion, and face mesmerize devotees, angels, devas, light beings, the higher celestials, as well as the dark and the demonic

12. whose flowing hair locks represent the descent of light and the mighty flow of the Ganges, Godavari, and the Yamuna rivers and whose ivory skin embarrasses even Lord Ganesh whose white tusks remain lackluster compared to her glow

13. whose ebullient laughter confuses us into thinking a babbling, cool, and refreshing brook is just a few footsteps away

14. who is the Supreme Goddess who suffered through countless births in all dimensions to be able to contain, bear, and bestow the infinite sacred inner light

15. who was born as an Avatar and whose unswerving love for Krishna left her broken-hearted and derelict, wandering and searching for her Divine reunion with her beloved

16. who rests in her own *Satchidananda Swarupa,* which is absolute truth, knowledge, and bliss

17. whose highest Soruba Samadhi was unbroken from her very childhood, and who spent weeks and months lost in the Divine Light in the Eternal Blue and in the Divine Play in the Ocean of Consciousness

18. who is divinely guided by Maha Avatar Babaji, Mother Mary, Christ, Krishna, Buddha, Shirdi Sai Baba, and countless other radiant beings, and who is near and dear to their cosmic mission for the enlightenment of planet Earth and other worlds

19. who is the channel through which the Divine avatars and beings of light constantly guide so mankind can receive their messages of hope and inspiration

20. who revels in the burning, ever-expanding radiant fire of Kundalini Yoga

21. who is a perfect Shambavi, Urdvaretri, and Urdvadrishti Siddha Yogini

22. who is none other than Ardha Nareshwari, the androgynous union of Shiva and Shakti

23. who enjoys perfect Nirvikalpa Samadhi and Sahaja Avastha, and bestows this state upon us through her Grace

24. who simultaneously exists, uplifts, and serves all in known and unknown spheres and dimensions

25. whose Samadhi state makes the three worlds tremble in awe and amazement

26. whose crown chakra radiates the power of millions of scintillating stars, suns, moons, comets, and galaxies

27. who has merged with the secret Blue Being and has exploded the inner Blue Pearl and Star

28. whose Grace pours out of her visuddha chakra -- the blue ocean of consciousness that embodies her sacred name

29. who resides in the hearts of our anahata and hridaya chakras in the form of our sacred Ishta Devata

30. who ignites our Solar Nadis and chakras through the power of her awakened Solar Light Body

31. whose awakened swadhishthana chakra sparks our creativity, procreative power, and innate wisdom

32. who playfully whispers into Ganesh's whimsical ears to remove obstacles within our chakra muladhar

33. who heroically and easily dispels fear through the wave of her hands and the rhythmic clicks of her nimble fingers

34. who rests in perfect cosmic and unity consciousness . . . and beyond

35. who escapes and yet has never been prisoner of time and space

36. who is born and unborn

37. who is omniscient, omnipotent, and omnipresent

38. who has transcended the three Gunas and has attained Shiva Consciousness

39. who has mastered the state of pure forgiveness and mercy

40. who has earned the attention and admiration of all the celestials

41. who respects all faiths and traditions, known and unknown, and in the seen and unseen worlds

42. who is the beloved of all her cherished devotees and speaks to them through the inner planes of the Divine

43. who has sacrificed her entire life and being on behalf of humanity under the auspices of the Divine Light

44. whose cosmic rays of love and compassion emanate everywhere to save and heal all sentient creatures and beings

45. whose grace magically falls upon the virtuous, as well as the wicked

46. who encourages self-effort along with begetting grace

47. who bestows perfect prosperity and abundance

48. who tirelessly sits for Darshan so we may know our inner self and glory

49. whose motherly Darshan embrace releases countless lifetimes of traumas, abuse, and misuse

50. whose asana and demeanor in Darshan resembles a living deity seated upon a temple altar of precious gold

51. whose consciousness dwells in myriad and multitudes of worlds at once, healing different orders of beings

52. who incessantly labors through prayers, affirmations, and healings for the sake of uplifting the world

53. who feels the suffering of mankind and all sentient beings within her own cosmic body

54. who immediately hears the woes of the impoverished and sends ethereal help to those who cry out from the wounds of their hearts

55. who dispels darkness and karma through mantras of love and light for those who are desperate, miserable, and physically ill

56. who patiently and painstakingly cleanses her devotees' families' karma of their ancestral lineages

57. who offers endless counsel to uniquely clean and clear away miseries and sorrows

58. who has consciously facilitated forgiveness prayers as a means to Sadhana and spiritual practice unto itself

59. who sees the world with equal vision, equanimity, and equipoise

60. whose inner joy and enthusiasm for service is unending and effortless

61. who takes special care of women, children, animals, plants, the elderly, renunciants, the destitute, and those with special needs

62. whose crown chakra is ever attracting higher, greater, and faster waves of light for the uplifting of light workers through the steadiness of Shambavi Mudra

63. who offers, mediates, and negotiates infinite prayer requests to the Para Atman Light for the benefit of all who sincerely ask

64. whose Seva Vision is to create Global Dharma Schools of Vedic Wisdom, Learning, Health, Medicine, and Healing

65. whose protective rays pour out from her ajna chakra to penetrate the darkness and shadow within our auric fields

66. who communes with the celestial physicians for the healing of those ill in body and mind, and whose electrifying touch heals the disease of the body and of worldly burden

67. who bestows boons to those who sincerely implore her through their purity of heart

68. whose inner Shakti enters our seven Dhatus or bodily tissues, thereby purifying them and making them whole and healed

69. who bestows pure Shaktipat -- the descent of Light, Love, and Grace through her look, touch, will, and word -- entering the seeker, taking residence in the heart, and awakening the Kundalini within

70. who is the Supreme Mistress of Yoga who initiates light workers into the subtle secrets of Ayurveda and Light Healing

71. whose Guru Sankalpa pierces the three Granthis or knots in muladhara, anahata, and ajna chakras

72. who, upon focus on her miraculous form, moves our minds to becomes one, eternal, pure, and still

73. who ferociously and victoriously upholds the auspiciousness and importance of fulfilling our sacred duties and missions upon planet Earth

74. who encourages the importance of regular spiritual practice through positive thoughts, words, deeds, choices, and actions

75. who never judges by harsh patriarchy; rather, co-creates with the free will of all who seek her guidance

76. who has merged into the cosmic light and sound to realize she is cosmic light and sound, and also beyond the primordial hum

77. who honors herself and by doing so honors all

78. who is friend, mother, sister, goddess, and great benefactress to all

79. who knows no difference between love and light, and through this power dispels all fears and negativity

80. who is immersed in the state of steady wisdom -- *Samanasya Parayana*

81. who fulfills all desires -- *Karma dhukayai*

82. who is Supreme Light -- *Param Arul Jyothi*

83. who is form and formless -- *Murta Amurta*

84. who abides in truth and is truth -- *Satya Vrata*

85. who is the mother of all beings -- *Janani Devi*

86. who is *Brahman*

87. who is the mother of the universe -- *Prasavitri*

88. who embodies the foundation and the manifestation of the Universe -- *Pratishtaya and Prakritic*

89. who is the mother of the valiant and best of devotees -- *Viramatre*

90. who gives salvation and is the abode of salvation -- *Mukunda Mukti Nilaya*

91. who is the knower of all thoughts and sentiments -- *Bhavajna*

92. who eradicates the disease of the cycles of birth and death -- *Bhava Roghini*

93. who rejoices when her devotees are liberated from the bonds of rebirth and death

94. who even transcends the state of peace -- *Santyatita Kalatmika*

95. who dwells in the highest state -- *Kartha*

96. who ends all sins and sorrows -- *Akantaya*

97. who is free from cause and effect -- *Karya Karana Nirmukta*

98. who is filled with undying compassion -- *Daya Karuna*

99. whose Grace knows no boundaries

100. who stands only for righteousness

101. who is the diadem of steadfastness -- *Stithya Prajna*

102. who is the master of discernment and dispassion -- *Viveka and Vairagya*

103. who has risen above likes and dislikes -- *Raga and Dvesha*

104. who laughs at the *Abini Vesha* or clever antics of the monkey mind

105. who is purely selfless, serving, and loving to all

106. who only wants the highest and best for all she serves

107. who is the Divine Mother among gurus and master of teachers

108. who is the Supreme Avatar of Love and Light

109 – 216

Salutations to the One:

109. who humbly discourages us to worship her by turning us directly to the Light of Para Atman to offer new ways and teachings during the dawn of the Golden Age

110. who is yet worthy of worship because she has merged into the Para Atman Light to become Para Atman

111. who is the source of inspiration to the four Kumaras: Sanandana, Sanakya, Sanat Kumara, and Sanatana

112. whom the Kumaras gain their eternal youth and vigor to share the secrets of enlightenment to innumerable worlds

113. who is none other than Bhaglamukhi, the supreme sovereign of justice and liberty, who arrests our enemies from spreading vice and evil

114. who conceals her divinity in human form as Yoga Maya veils the cosmic light from the eyes of mortals

115. who is Gayatri Devi, Mother of the Vedas, who emanates wisdom in the 12 sacred directions

116. who imbibes the energy of Meenakshi and Kamakshi Devi to remove worry and to fulfill our secret wishes

117. who is the ninth unknown manifestation of Suvarna Lakshmi, the Golden Queen, who bestows material fortune and spiritual attainment

118. who is the incarnation of Santoshi Devi, the Great Mother of contentment, laughter, humor, and joy

119. who is the eleventh secret Mahavidya, who is at the center of the red bindu of the Great Sri Vidya Yantra

120. who reflects the Divine attributes of Shodashi and the Divine synthesis of education, music, and power

121. who is the prana pratishta or great cosmic essence that resides within idols of stone and gem

122. who has silently helped over eons upon eons to purify the blood lines of Abraham, Ishmael, Isaiah, Isaac, Moses, and Jacob

123. whose Sankalpa or intention to us is unwavering, steady, and true

124. who revels and embodies the energy of Chidvilasa or the Divine Play of Consciousness

125. whose mind is always imbued and saturated with the sweetness of ambrosial nectar

126. who finds only good in seeming calamity

127. who inspires novices to become masters of themselves

128. who is like a lake's waves that have disappeared so we may see our own clear reflection upon her calm waters

129. who flows perfectly in Divine timing and order

130. whose lotus feet and hands are forever emanating rays of Chit Shakti

131. who is the power behind the mystery of Kala Bhairava and yet is beyond even his control of time and space

132. whose breath of fire in the form of Prana Shakti dispels mankind's ignorance or primordial avidya

133. whose power of Matrika Shakti, the energy and elocution behind words, baffles even the greatest scholars and orators

134. who summons the wrath of Kali and Durga when we face the frightening shadows of evil and void

OCEAN OF CONSCIOUSNESS

135. who dances in Radha Bhava, thinking only of the mesmerizing beauty of Sri Krishna, and whose beauty even makes him pause the play of his flute

136. who spontaneously instills pure selflessness through her Grace

137. who sits like a gentle butterfly upon the Buddha's shoulder to inspire his serenity and peace

138. who charms Lord Yama, the God of Death, to avert the premature demise of those near and dear

139. who fearlessly enters the worlds of Hell, the Patala Lokas, to rescue the fallen from certain suffering and eons of penance by her intercession of Grace

140. who veils her presence to silently watch and guide the actions of global light workers

141. who flies upon the wings of Grace to quickly feed the spiritual hunger of fledgling seekers

142. who is simultaneously everywhere and nowhere, and yet beyond both

143. whose dazzling smile is reflected within millions of raindrops and the morning dew

144. whose meritorious actions from countless births now make it easy for others to ascend into the Light

145. whose cosmic chanting reverberates in concentric circles, much like a pebble dropped into a crystalline pond

146. who fearlessly dispels demons, ghosts, goblins, and ghouls through her laughter and song

147. who is adored by fairies, devas, elves, gnomes, and sprites who adorn her with necklaces that sparkle and shine

148. whose hypnotizing voice leads us to the Divine sound, unlike the wicked Sirens whose song drove men to their destruction and death

149. whose light of blessing opens the inner doors of the heart like the Auroras and Ushas unlock the gates of the rising sun

150. whose benediction to global humanity brightly beams as the noon sun reaches its zenith

151. who gently caresses the face of mankind, much like the soft rays of the setting sun

152. who soothes the pain and cry of the heart, much like the coolness of the rising moon

153. who drenches raindrops of love upon the parched fields of the heart

154. who rides the sky's rainbows, holding the pot of golden knowledge to offer it to those who follow her to the end of the other side

155. whose endless patience even surpasses the fortitude of the Himalayas

156. who ascended from the lowest valleys of doubt and fear to reach the twin peaks of faith and trust

157. who knows the great mysteries of the Hawaiian Islands

158. who is immersed in pure ecstasy as she dances upon the shores of Kauai

159. who calms the wrath of the Goddess Pele to ease the islands' smoldering land and boiling sea

160. who calmly guides the world of cetaceans, inspiring them to swim and sing within Earth's troubled waters

161. who is respected by the Native Americans as the mother who lovingly descended from the Great Spirit

162. who lovingly upheld her ancient contract to the Meso and South Americans to help uplift and liberate many generations of natives

OCEAN OF CONSCIOUSNESS

163. who absorbs ancient tribal suffering to restore peace, forgiveness, and harmony to native lands

164. who fulfilled her promise to the native elders to restore and recall their ancient messages for the new Golden Age

165. who is the beloved daughter of Africa, and who uplifts and revives this sacred land to its previous glory and splendor

166. who lovingly guides us to the paradise beyond the other side of abandonment

167. whose flow of inner blood mirrors the flow of Earth's sacred rivers and waterfalls

168. whose mission is threefold: to awaken global humanity, to enlighten and inspire light workers, and to uplift her own earthly lineage

169. who is the sacred thread that leads and guides us out of the dark Minotaur's labyrinth into the freedom of the light of truth

170. who acts through pure Sattva, although she is beyond the three Gunas

171. whose lotus feet are embedded within the two hemispheres of the brain

172. who sits upon the guru's sandals secretly hidden within the sahasrar chakra

173. who is challenged to remain in body as the will of the Divine Light attempts to reclaim her brilliance

174. who covets the secrets of the Sahasrar to reveal them to worthy beings

175. who speaks without speaking, thinks without thinking, and acts without acting

176. whose petals of the heart bloom and blossom to create a fragrant inner bouquet of love, bliss, and peace

177. whose Divine ambrosia from the Heaven's showers down upon her chakras and splashes upon those who surround themselves in her presence

178. who dances upon and within the mysteries of the inner Blue Pearl

179. who rides inside the vehicle of the inner Blue Star to travel and give council to beings who call upon her

180. who revels in and channels the light and power from the central sun

181. who has mastered sleepless sleep

182. whose mind is transfixed upon her own unending radiance

183. who effortlessly conveys herself to travel between and within each and every dimension and sphere

184. who easily rides the inner column of light above the Sahasrar to realms beyond the beyond

185. whose day becomes night and whose night becomes day

186. who appears as mortal, knowing she is comprised of scintillating particles of light and waves of sound

187. whose global mission has been foreseen as the rishis fix their inner gaze upon her blue feminine form

188. who plays hide and seek within the deep cavernous meditation of cloistered yogis

189. who is fully aware of innumerable worlds born and destroyed within a blink of her eyes

190. whose power and Grace surpasses that of a 1008 gurus and beyond

191. who enters the dream state of those who draw her close to their hearts

192. whose inner luster is ever glowing from the golden chambers of her awakened heart

193. whose cosmic mind is creating and manifesting unending miracles

194. whose power of words (Matrika Shakti) are the mantras that soften even the most hardened of minds

195. whose words of foreknowledge manifest into the lives of her devotees

196. who restores luminosity into the eyes of the forsaken

197. whose tears for this suffering world become the cherished emollient to apply for healing and health

198. who restores and consoles Nature's five elements: Vayu, Agni, Bhoomi, Jala, and Akasha

199. who averts and attenuates natural calamities agitated by the wicked actions of sleeping humanity

200. who painstakingly bears the burden of humanity's sorrows and misdeeds

201. whose light workers channel her Shakti for the evolution of the New Golden Age

202. who offers priceless counsel to those who are evolving their planetary missions

203. who feels the pain and cry of animals mercilessly slaughtered for food, fun, and feast

204. whose mere presence knowingly and unknowingly transforms sentient and insentient beings

205. who is ever growing and expanding even from her own infinite consciousness

206. whom the impossible becomes possible

207. who upholds dharma in the face of temptation from the dark

208. who inspires students through the activation of the Vak Nadi at the tips of their tongues

209. who is simultaneously guiding many within other dimensions while teaching Earth beings in her physical form

210. who is the inspiration behind the science of life -- *Ayur-Veda*

211. who heals without healing, cures without curing, and restores without restoring

212. who inspires Earth's leaders from the past, present, and future

213. who is reuniting Twin Flames, High Flames, and Soul Mates to remember their sacred soul contracts with each other and the world

214. who offers endless counsel to householders afflicted by the turmoil and disease of worldly affliction

215. who revels in delight to protect and guide monastic austerities

216. who is offering transformation to countless millions to shift old paradigms and beliefs

OCEAN OF CONSCIOUSNESS

217 – 324

Salutations to the One:

217. who exudes the spiritual fragrance of 1008 lotus blossoms that cause honeybees to swarm and swoon around her exalted essence

218. whose luminous form attracts fireflies to shine their light as they perform aarti around her radiant being

219. who acknowledges that time is our greatest friend and yet our greatest enemy

220. who experiences that change is the only constant in this dualistic world

221. who is lost in the love unions of Radha and Krishna and Rama and Sita, knowing their unity is felt within the swirling bliss of heart and soul

222. who laments having to descend into a day of earthly burden after a cloaked night spent in ecstatic bliss

223. who is known as Lalithananda, the royal matron who revels in the universal sport of creation and dissolution

224. who is the cosmic seamstress, untying the cords and knots that bind our consciousnesses to the material realm

225. who easily enters the Akasha records to revamp and remold the destiny of those who seek forgiveness

226. who is the Divine conqueror of the forgotten, forbidden, and unexplored lands within the heart

227. who is courageous at traversing unending worlds that have no beginning or end

228. who lovingly rests her head upon the shoulders of those who ponder her, if only for a second's fraction

229. who knows that real art lies in the heart and that heart contains the essence of art

230. who is a perfect Shrotiya, the one who knows how to balance the spiritual with the worldly

231. who blesses unseen beings who surround our world to guide and protect Mother Earth

232. who is aware of unknown, unspoken ethereal languages dampened from the ears of mortals

233. who silently offers wakeful forgiveness prayers to the Light on behalf of sleeping humanity

234. who knows all that is, was, and ever will be is comprised of light, bliss, and love

235. who always lives in cosmic love rooted within the primordial Source

236. who is none other than Arulananda, the sparkling damsel of luminous, blissful light

237. who is known as Hamsananda, the graceful maiden who softly assumes the qualities of the discerning swan

238. who is the Goddess Uma Devi, the mesmerizing beauty who captures the crescent moon within her hair and fastens the stars upon her crown

239. whose love is the reason why the caterpillar patiently slumbers to become the butterfly

240. who is the tenacious inspiration behind the baby bird's drive to peck out of its shell

241. who is detached and yet attached, attached but not detached, and detached and yet not detached

242. who is forever mindful of those who think of her and of those who yet do not ponder her mysteries

243. who is the author of our dreams, hopes, and aspirations

244. whose strength of Shaktipat can be as mighty as the beats of the eagles' wings or as soft and quiet as the wispy wing beats of the tiny hummingbird

245. who takes 100,008 steps toward us as we take one step towards her

246. who seeks to console rather than to be consoled

247. who offers to serve rather than to be served

248. who gives and yet is not the giver, and who receives and is yet not the receiver

249. who is Kriyavati, the primordial cause for kriyas within bodies and minds

250. who is the original source for the upward process of Urdvaretra Shakti

251. whose gaze is above and beyond the Shambavi Mudra

252. who has overcome and endured all forms of kriyas

253. who reflects our brilliant Istha Devata inside the diamond of the heart

254. who destroys our prarabdha, sanchita, and agami karmas

255. whose Grace nullifies and cancels the need for rebirth

256. who has mastered and blended the many forms of love into one sacred Love

257. who is the tiny sprout underneath the boulder of ego that causes its crack and crumble

258. who is always centered in Higher Self by transcending the Lower Self

259. whose Samadhi state is uninterrupted by the chaos of this world

260. who is the cosmic rescuer for those who are tossed about by the torrential storms of delusion

261. whose words echo and resound like the Goddess Vajreshwari whose thunderous Nada strikes the sadhaka's heart

262. whose face resembles the deep, eerie blackness of pregnant cloud bursts as Kali Bhava rumbles through her being

263. whose Divine prana transmitted during Shaktipat razzle and dazzle the unawakened to become awakened

264. who is Aurora Rani, the lustrous monarch whose luminous glow is comprised of Ojas Shakti

265. who resides in the yellow bone marrow as Mej Ojas and is the primal fuel for meditation and prayer

266. whose compassionate glance attracts birds and beasts to rest upon her bosom

267. who has brought down the restoration and the remembrance of the Divine Feminine on planet Earth

268. who balances male and female within the body, mind, and Self for us to realize that we are beyond polarity

269. who offers healing to the disempowered female within man and woman

270. who is uplifting and encouraging women and men to embrace their forgotten feminine power

271. whose feminine inspiration causes the resurgence of respectful chivalry

272. who honors natural child birth and the energy of menses, Apana Shakti, or downward flow

273. who honors the menstrual blood as an integral element of Mother Earth, reviving its meaning from the ancient world

274. who is behind the force of life within the developing womb

275. who sends compassion to the soul trapped inside the confines of the womb

276. whose delicate blessings nurture and guard the growing, innocent womb

277. who is a master at balancing the Ida and Pingala nadis so male and female energy is whole and healed

278. who is Saraswati Devi, the one who teaches not but is forever learning

279. whose constant smile is reflected in the smile of the dolphin's charming play

280. who sees unity in diversity and diversity in unity

281. who plays like the fool before the vain and the wicked, and yet is an empress of wisdom before the innocent and the pure

282. who knows but does not tell, and who pretends to not know and yet still does not tell

283. whose love we cannot die without, and yet, with her love, we can finally die

284. whose love we cannot live without and yet, with her love, we cannot die

285. who knows all paths are rainbow rays that lead back to the Supreme White Light

286. who is none other than Annapoorneshwari, the generous, bountiful cornucopia of food and harvest

287. who is Sadapoorna and who has taken a Sankalpa to eradicate the poverty of food in this unbalanced world

288. who feels the hunger of starving children within her own being and dies along with them to escort them to Heaven

289. who is a perfect Poorna Yogini who knows only fullness rather than lack

290. who is forever destroying Shakti Daridriya or the disease of poverty consciousness

291. who cannot rest through any century until mankind fully enlightens

292. who is none other than Dhumavati, the Divine crone or hag who meditates in graveyards and pyres to liberate Earthbound souls

293. who acts without thinking and thinks without acting

OCEAN OF CONSCIOUSNESS

294. who attracts without attracting, yet with attraction attracts

295. who remains inwardly as a child to the Light of Para Atman

296. who is forever planting vital seeds for the heart's golden harvest

297. who inspires all to uncover, discover, and recover

298. who illumines the shadowy eclipse of the heart

299. who encourages all to make quilts as life gives them scraps

300. who is aware that true health is wealth and that true wealth is enlightenment

301. who is the dearest of the dear to the Avatars of the East

302. who is nearest to the near to the Saints and Masters of the West

303. who is beloved by the Gods of the North

304. who is cherished and adored by the Devas of the South

305. whose one pointed Samadhi with the Divine far surpasses Arjuna's inability to bear and contain the Swaroopa state

306. who humbly bows in all the sacred directions as the servant to all

307. who bears the karma of the master the disciples create out of their own ignorance, yet loving innocence

308. who is silently working to create enlightened forms of rule and order

309. who is dissolving harsh patriarchal fear and control

310. who has sacrificed the personal for the sake of service

311. who rests under the coolness of the Hawaiian moon and the calmness of the breeze to fulfill a myriad prayers

312. who teaches enlightenment is not possible without forgiveness

313. who wears a necklace of endless numbers of pearls of meritorious deeds

314. whose silent reverberation and reverberating silence is experienced after passing through the Shabda sounds

315. whose presence is where we find eternal rest after hearing the conch, bell, nightingale, drum, flute, bagpipes, harp, and thunder

316. who dances in Divinity as she divinely dances

317. who knows today's enemy is tomorrow's friend

318. who is the communicating bridge for interstellar beings

319. who is the great ambassador for the extraterrestrials of Light and Love

320. who lovingly lives to die and dies to live for the sake of suffering souls

321. who is quietly serene and serenely quiet

322. who is golden silence, silently golden, and the gold ore of silence

323. who lovingly transforms all deep within the sacred catacombs of silence

324. who all the Yogi kings and pharaohs of yester-year and yore cry out from their tombs for to beseech her to save this world from disease and despair

OCEAN OF CONSCIOUSNESS

325 - 432

Salutations to the One:

325. who is Vishudananda, and who floats upon the blue ocean of consciousness inside her own bubble of bliss

326. who is guiding and guarding this world with 1,000,008 hands, eyes, heads, and weapons

327. who is the primordial creatrix

328. who is watched by 108,000 ethereal rishis who surround her being while performing rituals for the success of her mission

329. who is the ebb and flow of the Hawaiian tide as the moon rises and sets from dusk to dawn

330. who knows in reality the body and mind do not exist

331. who is known as Muktananda Devi, the mother of blissful liberation

332. who spreads a royal banquet of delicious delicacies of spiritual practices for all to enjoy

333. whose three-starred bindi upon her brow represents the three gunas we must transcend

334. who covets the secret siddhis to use as Divine tools for change

335. who knows all of her past, present, parallel present, and future births

336. who could not bear the worldly antics and attitudes or clatter and chatter of her early schooling

337. whose family fought and feuded over her seeming madness

338. who was a stranger and was estranged from her own family and friends

339. whose burning quest for the Light brought her to India, the land of the gods

340. who was initiated by rare Avatars of the East who recognized her Divine state and mission

341. who wandered along the shores of Goa frustrated and despairing for the longing of Divine Union

342. who spent sleepless nights burning in the desire for total merging with truth

343. who was prepared to die on heated stones by the restless sea unless Para Atman revealed his true form

344. who then heard a Divine whisper to return to her quarters

345. who — lo and behold! — exploded into the Divine Vishva Swaroopa in humble quarters

346. who painstakingly bore the shocking swoon of pure Arula, omniscience, omnipresence, and omnipotence, while attempting to function in a limited frame

347. whose crippled body almost perished as it attempted to bear the highest Light

348. who knew no boundary between herself and the eternal blue of consciousness

349. who fought with guides and guidance to ascend back into Light, but was commanded to return to transmit Light to awaken global humanity

350. who learned to contain the entire cosmos within her being while functioning in body and mind

351. who finally returned to normal body and mind for the benefit of humanity and to help share what she discovered

352. whose Samadhi state culminated through countless lives spent in meditation, penance, practice, and prayer

353. whose mission humbly commenced with small counsels and healing

354. who refused to accept offers to head spiritual lineages so she could teach others direct access to Para Atman

OCEAN OF CONSCIOUSNESS

355. who obtained counsel and vision to move to the West

356. who received this command from a Divine being who manifested before her

357. who humbly sought her own mentorship to learn and recall the power of forgiveness prayers

358. whose trust in the Divine Light ever expands her global mission

359. who surrendered to Para Atman to form her mission's foundation of truth

360. whose two auspicious eyebrows resemble double rainbows of many hues

361. whose smile is curved like the crescent moon

362. who radiates the golden sun inside her spiritual eye

363. who sees the Star of David twinkling in the firmament of the Sahasrar

364. who knows the Star of the East is within the pineal and pituitary glands

365. who knows the history and mystery of Jesus' sojourn in the land of the Hindus

366. who knows the secret story of the demise of Atlantis and Lemuria

367. who tirelessly works on the negative ego of man to avert the fate of destruction ancient Atlantis faced

368. who recognizes many Earth humans are star-seeded beings

369. who sees humans incarnate between the physical and astral, who are trapped within this limiting prison

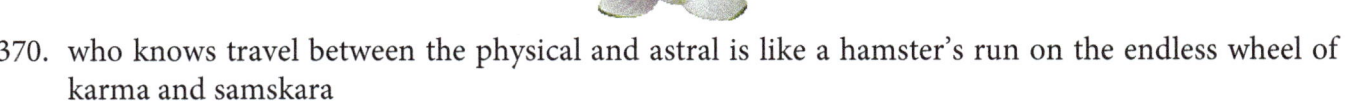

370. who knows travel between the physical and astral is like a hamster's run on the endless wheel of karma and samskara

371. who seeks to liberate souls from the astral and physical into the timeless consciousness of the Para Atman light

372. who guides us to transcend even the Great Void

373. who knows we rest in the Void unaware the Light of Para Atman is still yet beyond

374. who constantly battles demons and devils that attempt to ensnare souls into the low astral spheres

375. whose private counsel is her unique gift to humanity

376. whose light transmission sessions are her offerings to light workers

377. whose vision lies in radical change and enlightenment in the new Golden Age

378. who sends inspiration to scientists, doctors, and engineers

379. who transmits creative ideas to those in the humanities

380. who silently seeks change in global law and government

381. who teaches true mother and fatherhood through the remembrance of Divine Feminine and Masculine

382. who works behind vaults for the redistribution of prosperity and wealth

383. who knows the secrets of harnessing new energy forms

384. who uplifts nations of poverty by raising awareness in those forgotten and forsaken lands

385. who envisions Golden Age medicine will heal through Divine Light

386. who raises mass consciousness to match off-world planets that are high and whole

387. who inspires the young and the eager to discover natural living

388. who smiles with glee when young souls embrace mantra and prayer

389. who enters the minds of naturalists to create restorative projects for the balance of life

390. who inspires Naturopaths of the East and West to rediscover the powerful properties of healing plants

391. whose outspoken wisdom inspires youthful minds to invent harmless technologies

392. who knows technology without spirituality only leads to a civilization's demise

393. who opens the gates and unlocks the doors for those also destined for global missions

394. who contracts with beings prior to birth to fulfill their destinies for the sake of humanity

395. who transforms old paradigm beliefs, thoughts, and practices

396. who replaces old beliefs and patterns with constructive insight and wisdom

397. who is restoring the pathless path

398. who enlightens new Siddhas, Savants, Masters, and Sages to guide humanity in the Golden Age

399. who recognizes the plight of modern suffering rooted in the disease of loneliness and lack of love

400. who works endlessly to preserve dying species of flora and fauna

401. who appeals to Mother Earth to forgive mankind's abuse of her sacred home

402. who awakens millions to realize that Mother Earth, Bhoomi Devi, is a living, conscious being

403. who Mother Gaia is forever grateful to as she is being guarded and healed

404. who is a master surgeon, excising the cancer of negative ego

405. who is an expert physician whose Divine emollient dissolves the disease of negativity

406. who applies the cosmic salve of healing light to soothe the agitated minds of the psychotic and the deranged

407. who works to calm and to appease angered devas of nature and nurture

408. who knows the secret of sending light to attenuate the agitation of natural elements

409. whose darshan often takes on the karma of seekers to send back to the Light

410. who is unaffected by others' negative karma through her shielding by the Light

411. who works with those who see the Divine as light

412. who knows there is no separation between Divine Light and Love just as there is no difference between particle and wave

413. who is the guiding lighthouse helping navigate the treacherous waters of modern living

414. who is the antithesis of violence and vanity

415. who resonates with those who are authentic and genuine, while ignoring those who remain wicked and vain

416. who carries those trapped upon the surface waves of criticism and judgment to the calm deep waters of understanding and compassion

417. who is the Divine spelunker safely guiding us to explore the black cavernous recesses of heart and mind

OCEAN OF CONSCIOUSNESS

418. who knows lighting one candle of hope dispels eons of darkness within mind and heart

419. who is Raja Rajeswari, the mother of queenly virtues

420. whose smile and giggle is only the iceberg's tip of her ebullient joy

421. who is the synthesis of protective energy from the six warrior goddesses: Kali, Subadra, Durga, Pratyangira, Chamundi, and Dhari Devi

422. who is the integral blend of Lakshmis, Dhana, Gaja, Adhi, Santhana, Aishwarya, Vijaya, Veera and Dhanya

423. who bears the power of Maha or Sundara Lakshmi

424. who encompasses the 108 forms of Saraswati Devi

425. who is the Amazonian Warrior Goddess, piercing the heart with bow and arrow to allow love to bleed through a seeker's being

426. who is the high temple priestess whose worship consists of the highest prayers to the Light

427. who is the African lady shamanic who knows the art of natural healing

428. who is the aboriginal medicine woman who knows how to harness the guarded powers of the Lands of Bush

429. who is the Bodhi Sattva, upholding respect for elders and ancestors

430. who is the revered feminine expressed through the sacred Native American white buffalo calf

431. who is the forgotten goddess power in the Islamic world that covered her behind darkened cloths of cloak and veil

432. who is the song of sorrow, yet strength, of poor black women locked in despair but hopeful in heart

OCEAN OF CONSCIOUSNESS

433 – 540

Salutations to the One:

433. whose meditation imbibes effortless effort and spontaneous spontaneity

434. who is beyond Jivan Mukta, Siddha, Avadoota, and Arhat

435. who can never be accused of dereliction of duty

436. who is the sacred spark that ignites the forest fire of the heart

437. whose modaka or Divine archetypal vehicle is the playful dolphin

438. whose dolphin modaka represents the joyous, sprightly, and humorous nature of the Divine

439. who knows the dolphin is a being of pure oneness, happiness, and bliss

440. whose one look, one touch, one word, one thought, and one deed is enough to transform an entire lifetime

441. whose touch upon a seeker's heart is as soft as rose petals

442. whose gaze upon seeker's being manifests spontaneous tears

443. whose words create the remembrance of the primordial hum

444. whose thoughts directed toward this world create wave upon wave of Divine remembrance of Self

445. who cannot rest, but is ever at rest

446. whose white, silver, and gold garments flow with the winds of change

447. whose Shaktipat or descent of Grace can be as gentle as a baby's breath

448. whose prana can be felt like a zephyr wind

449. whose transmission of Grace can be cooling like the gentle breeze or as icy as the polar waters

450. whose mysterious energy can be experienced as the hot, blowing desert winds

451. whose Maha or Supreme Shaktipat can be fiery like the dragon's breath

452. who knows the mystery of the 27 forms of Shaktipat or transmissions of Grace

453. who is the cosmic hurricane whose gale force winds bring transformational change through flood and fury

454. who can incinerate the karma of lifetime after lifetime through the fiery furnace of blazing yoga

455. who people stand for hours to wait for her Darshan because they have endured countless eons to be in the presence of the living goddess

456. who compassionately bears the ignorance of those who misunderstand her mission

457. who sits on the throne of mercy to bear the insults of the world with complete equanimity and equipoise

458. who remains tranquil and serene despite the cruel agitation of the world

459. who seeks no praise but with whom praise seeks her

460. whose childhood was spent playing with inner guides, masters, angels, and gods

461. who innocently thought mankind was consciously experiencing this same kind of play

462. who was often taken by guides to travel by night to many and varied inner realms

463. who in childhood was surrounded by masters and mothers who would protect her slumber

464. who activates and is contained within the red body known as Rakteswari

465. who scintillates and is iridescent within the white body or Sveteshwari

466. who is the prime movement within the inky black body known as Krishneshwari

467. who activates and awakens a seeker's inner blue body or the Neela Purusha

468. whose Grace allows us to penetrate the five spiritual eyes to reach the final inner Sahasrar road

469. whose Grace no one can walk the higher Sahasrar path without

470. who activates Dakhini Devi, the Red Mercurial Goddess, fused with Brahma inside Muladara to ground seekers upon earth

471. who reveals Rakhini Devi or Venus, the Orange Goddess, mirror of Vishnu who lives in Swadisthana to create the flow of water within a seeker's being

472. who stirs and awakens Lakhini Devi, the Golden Yellow Goddess, burning with Mars and Agni, ignites the Self through brimstone and flame

473. who enlivens Kakini Devi or Artemis who, along with Isa and Jupiter, represent the free blowing wind within the green forests of Anahata

474. who breathes life through Sakina Devi and merged with Sada Shiva is the Saturnian air and wind of the vast Visuddha sky

475. who blossoms Hakini Shiva Devi or Athen, the darkest of night's deepest Uranian indigo behind the vast canopy of inner stars

476. who is none other than Parama Shiva who radiates Neptunian white, violet, and gold light beyond the five elements within the Sahasrar

OCEAN OF CONSCIOUSNESS

477. who is the primordial shudder and shake, allowing us
478. to hear the sounds lam, vam, ram yam ham ksham, and Aum deep within the inner vortices

479. who is the tiny salt doll who sauntered into the sea to become the limitless ocean

480. who is the jewel clip upon Sikh masters' turbans that bind their silks around their heads

481. who is like a tiny drop of sea water that contains the entire ocean

482. who reveals more of her inner being as she opens more of a devotee's inner heart

483. who lovingly feeds spiritual nourishment spoon by spoon to our innocent, growing hearts and minds

484. who is the cosmic puppeteer animating our bodies and beings

485. who is the clever ventriloquist breathing wind and word into the power of speech

486. who is the master artist whose vast palette of colors paint the heart's canvas

487. who is the kaleidoscope of hues through which we perceive the myriad rays and patterns of Divine Light

488. who is the Supreme Master Psychic and Psychic Master

489. who is the soul's sole soul

490. who is like an unwavering candle that slowly melts to give others light

491. who restores the remembrance of Unity Consciousness to those who choose conscious unity

492. whose cooling moonbeams provide an illumined path through the thick forests of the darkened mind

493. who is shy and demure, yet bold and brazen as the many moods of the Goddess Chiti Shakti

494. who is Goddess Kundalini rising from within the virtuous, and yet who falls within those who are wicked

495. whose pastel colored shades suffuse and infuse the firmaments of the Sahasrar

496. who pierces the doorway to total absoluteness within the 8th lotus of our inner beings

497. whose billowing, smoky clouds spill into the realms of Self

498. whose shy, tiny, quiet voice of intuition and guidance may be heard inside the right ear

499. who releases ambrosial nectar that showers upon the inner tongue like a fresh torrential downpour

500. whose nature as the Goddess Hemagiri Nandini is to merge with all as much as she longs to merge with Shiva

501. who has been slumbering at the base of the spine for countless eons upon eons, and centuries upon centuries

502. who is stirred from her slumber by the will and pure Grace of the Divine Light

503. whose serpent power that ascends is no different than the Divine Grace that descends

504. who acknowledges that civilizations perish when they do not open the heart equally to that of the mind

505. who claims nothing because she has merged into pure nothingness

506. whose often eccentric and mysterious words, actions, thoughts, and guidance cannot be grasped by the limited mind

507. who has the power of Divya-Dristhi, the one who perfectly guides outcomes and issues

508. who is the only one who truly cares about our inner sorrows and pains

509. who is forever youthful and ageless, yet is constantly aging and decaying

510. whose will not even an atom can move without

511. who comprises the atom itself and whose ultimate essence is that of pure love

512. who is pure fullness and whose fullness remains full even if seemingly removed

513. who advises to never point a finger because in doing so four other fingers are always pointing back

514. whose one outstretched hand is forever receiving while the other is always giving

515. who is constantly grounded in Abhaya Mudra with one hand pointing to the Heavens while the other is pointing to Earth

516. who meditates in Chin Mudra, which invokes the infinity symbol of creation that has no beginning or end

517. who is Yoga Mudra, the Great Seal of Yoga

518. whose spellbinding gestures in Darshan are animated by Kundalini herself

519. who is the hot, blowing steam that evaporates above the surface of the boiling waters of our spiritual pursuits

520. who is the smoldering cauldron of lotions and potions in which magical white light incantations are offered to benefit the world

521. who is the White Light Sorceress forever casting her spell to awaken and remember

522. who runs and eludes if we pursue, but pursues those who stop running

523. whose upward movement within the sap of trees parallels the Kundalini's inner flow

524. who is the sky's crystal blue star upon which we make wishes and share hopes, dreams, and aspirations

525. who is beyond the childish use of the Merkabah vehicle for travel between dimensions

526. who is Narayani, the beloved daughter of the solar dynasties and deities

527. whose mind lives in heart and whose heart lives in mind

528. who knows the highest gratitude manifests the right attitude

529. who hears even the footsteps of the little ant

530. who understands this solar system is but a tiny atom in the entire cosmos

531. who becomes a child in front of a child

532. who is child-like but not childish

533. who realizes to face change one must change face

534. who walks the razor's edge

535. who sees without seeing, hears without hearing, speaks without speaking, feels without feeling, and tastes without tasting

536. who is silence behind the unstruck sounds

537. who is the tree of life that grows upside down, representing the descent of Grace

538. who is the one elephants raise their trunks to offer her bouquets of flowers

OCEAN OF CONSCIOUSNESS

539. who knows the secret art and science of releasing the past and altering the future to create the harmonious NOW

540. who is favored by the animal deities

541. Who is the elusive fountain of youth pursued by many outer conquests and campaigns that did not realize she cleverly hides inside a person's very being

PEMMARAJU RAO

541 - 648

Salutations to the One:

542. whose intoxicating fragrance of peace far surpasses bouquets of fresh jasmines, gardenias, and lilies of the valley

543. who is pregnant with knowledge, creativity, and wisdom

544. who is the umbrella of protection from the hailstorms of life

545. who cuts through the illusion, confusion, and delusion of Maya

546. who cannot be influenced by the dark because she has realized it is only the absence of light

547. who knows darkness is still merely another form of light

548. who is the prime minister of the Universe

549. who is the prime director behind ethereal councils

550. who negotiates with ethereal councils and boards on our behalf

551. who cannot be limited to body and mind

552. who attained liberation many lifetimes ago

553. who thus has the capacity to liberate others now and in the future

554. who never attained liberation because there was nothing to liberate

555. who is free forever and is forever free

556. who is tethered to body and mind like a flying kite tied to a boulder

557. who rises above the canopy of the forest and is never lost among the trees

558. who is the calm Divine Eye in the center of the hurricane of life and living

559. who celebrates the ascent of Kauai into the fifth dimension

560. who longs for the entire world to ascend and evolve

561. who communes with other masters to expand the consciousness of mass humanity

562. who is the terrifying roar of an impending tornado that awakens our humility toward Mother Nature's power

563. who understands the essential link between spirituality and science

564. whose healing prayers create a platinum shield around seekers and savants

565. who easily repairs the pain and misery of aura tears within the light body

566. who is working with many to enhance and enliven the ethereal light body

567. who understands the ascension method of Jesus is available to all

568. who is aware Earth humans are not as awakened as other off-world humans and other beings

569. who respects all off-world planetary cultures

570. who gives Darshan to humans as well as non-humanoid sentient beings

571. who knows there are more off-world civilizations than there are sand grains along the seas

572. who knows planets, solar systems, stars, and galaxies are merely pinpoints of light against the vastness of infinity

573. who knows there is life in unknown forms that exists beyond human knowledge

574. Who offers Darshan to all kinds of extraterrestrial beings

575. who knows the secret origins of dolphins and penguins

576. who knows the star origins of the African animals

577. who knows the languages of birds and beasts

578. who respects all gurus, yogis, masters, divine mothers, saints, savants, rishis, and mendicants of all planets and places

579. who cherishes all teachers and all paths

580. who never judges or comments on any other spiritual path

581. who remains neutral and silent on the works of other teachings

582. who knows planets and stars are living beings

583. who knows intelligent life exists on other planets within the solar system

584. who offers appropriate pranams to temple deities of all paths, knowing the essence of the deity exists within its form

585. who understands the balance and importance behind ritual and non-ritualistic worship

586. who knows the masters and Divine beings of planets near and far

587. who is surrounded by her own lineage of light who are constantly guiding and guarding her mission

588. who walks the careful tight rope of destroying but not creating any new karma

589. who is a catalyst to bring higher healing and enlightening frequencies that have never entered Earth's planetary sphere

590. who laughs at the cosmic joke that there is really nothing to achieve or attain

591. who concedes that all deities from myriad worlds are the Divine infinite sparks of the one Light

592. who validates the integral synthesis of all forms of yoga

593. who understands the fundamental principle that restraint of the modifications of the mind is the foundation of yoga

594. who is a perfect Jnana Yogini

595. who is a master Bhakta Yogini

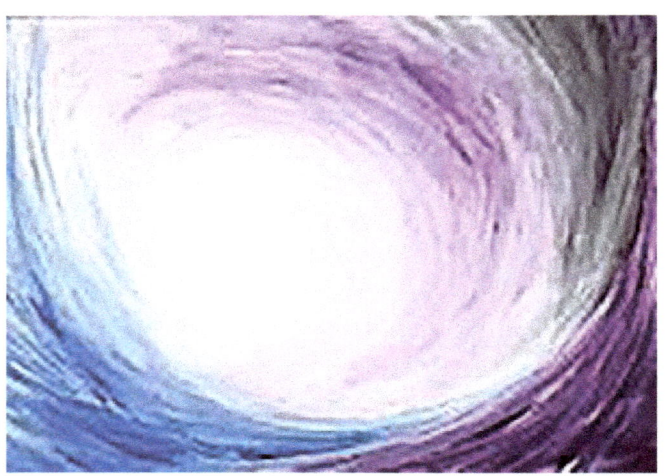

596. who shows by living example the practice of being an ideal Karma Yogini

597. who is the Supreme Raja Yogini who is even above the process of meditation

598. who is a Mantra Japa Yogini behind the energy and power of word and sound

599. who is a Hatha Yogini who performed all postures spontaneously in prior births through the awakened Shakti Kundalini

600. who is surrounded by millions of golden orbs and bubbles, each containing a deva of blessing and love

601. who is a cosmic comet that visits and graces a world only once in thousands, or perhaps millions of years

602. whose sacred tongue is forever chanting the mantras of Light

603. whose iridescent eyes constantly emit rays of chiti shakti

604. whose handsome nose is forever inhaling and exhaling cosmic light

605. whose awakened ears hear Divine nada sounds

606. whose pure tongue and lips speak only the truth

607. whose sacred touch feels and appreciates the gift of life and living

608. who has the blessings of the South Indian Siddhas of Light

609. who has the respect of the North Indian Masters of Love

610. who has the benediction of the East Indian Masters of Peace

611. who has the positive Sankalpa from the West Indian Masters of Power

612. who is supremely aware of the Divine sounds "A, KA, THA" that reverberate within the triangle of her Sahasrar

613. who is constantly focused on the guru's sandals within the inner triangle of the upper Sahasrar

614. who knows how to explode one's inner Blue Pearl in Divine timing and order

615. who is guiding many to become non-regressing Bodhi Sattvas

616. who is working on many for this incarnation to be their last earthly sojourn

617. whose company worldly people feel awkward and confused by, unable to bear her Divine energy and power

618. who was the energy of the soft green moss on the northern sides of trees that guided black southern slaves to the freedom of the north

619. who silently works to awaken, liberate, and integrate the peoples of the land of South Africa

620. who sleeps little, speaks, little, eats little, and drinks little in order to have more time to serve others

621. who honors the Middle Path

622. who, as she places her feet in the sea, tearfully remembers she must remain a prisoner of body away from the ocean of light until her mission is completed and fulfilled

623. who is the cosmic comedienne and clown who invokes laughter and song even among the most depressed and discouraged

624. who is a master at liberating one from the burden of demonic possession

625. who hears the cries and feels the pains of wounded soldiers dying on the battlefield

626. who knows how to optimally redraft a devotee's earthly blueprint for a better life design

627. who has the knowledge of Grace and is gracefully knowledgeable

628. whose Divine mission is not a labor of love, but rather a passionate love

629. who is known as Madhuri Devi, who oozes nectarean, blissful honey, from every pore of her being

630. who shatters the notion the sky is the limit, knowing limitlessness is beyond even the sky

631. who has pierced the veil of illusion and delusion

632. who cannot be fooled or swayed by false praise and admiration

OCEAN OF CONSCIOUSNESS

633. whose fathomless depths can never be totally measured

634. whose infinite heights can never be fully reached

635. whose length and breadth can never be wholly traversed or traveled

636. whose tiny, tinkling bells upon her anklets may be heard through the breeze as she takes her early morning walk with the rising sun

637. who is known, heard, and felt like the invisible but tangible blowing wind

638. who rescues the stranded disciples tethered and tangled by Savikalpa Samadhi into the tranquility of the hot-aired balloon of Sahaja Samadhi

639. whose life is a constant sacrifice and by whose penance creates a constant life

640. whose sunlight and rain fall equally upon the wise as well as the wicked

641. who radiates burning rays in all directions but is never scorched by her own brilliance

642. who knows the burning bush manifests as the awakened light of the inner Sahasrar

643. who is the eternal elixir of the Holy Grail

644. who is the Sun Goddess for whom the sunflower lovingly turns its head from East to West

645. who experiences that God is simple but everything else is complex

646. whose Shakti is potential in the unawakened just as fire is latent in wood

647. who smoothens away the dryness and cracks of negativity with the lotion of purity

648. who fills the dry, desolate dust bowl of the heart with cooling and drenching rains

649. who protectively embraces the world with her angelic wings

OCEAN OF CONSCIOUSNESS

649 - 756

Salutations to the One:

650. who compassionately continues to feed the hand that bites to those reptilians and other dark characters who bite the hand that feeds

651. who has sacrificed her entire life into the sacred yagna fires of dispassion and discrimination -- *Viveka* and *Vairagya*

652. who is free like the blowing breeze on a fresh spring day

653. whose work can never be halted

654. who distills the essence of the scriptures into that which can easily be grasped

655. who has experienced that which is written in scripture and lore

656. who is Somayajini, the one who knows the secrets of extracting Soma from the sacred inner spaces and from ritualistic fires

657. who is Agnihotrini, the one who understands the essence and benefit of Vedic fire rituals

658. who has performed countless rituals on behalf of humanity

659. whose length of time spent in meditation can never be mastered or measured

660. who has no fear of death because she "dies daily"

661. whose energy signature is unique in the world and among Avatar beings

662. whose seed of Shaktipat planted in us contains the entire essence of enlightenment, just as a buried acorn seedling one day becomes the mightiest of oak trees

663. whose meditation rests solely and one-pointedly on others' happiness

OCEAN OF CONSCIOUSNESS

664. who understands the disease of poverty and loneliness exists as lack of love, as well as the absence of basic necessities

665. who is Bindu Bhedini, the one whose Shakti has the power to pierce the optical chakras

666. who is Karna Bhedini, the energy of Kundalini who gifts the opening of the auricular chakras

667. who is Rudra Granthi Bhedini, the one whose has merged with the Goddess Kundalini to pierce the Brahma Granthi or knot at the base of the spine

668. who is Vishnu Granthi Bhedini, the one who pierces the knot of the heart so that Kundalini Devi can ascend to higher spheres

669. who is Rudra Granthi Bhedini whose power pierces the spiritual eye or point between the eyebrows

670. who is favored by Nandi, the Divine Cow, at the base of Visuddha or throat, who allows no one to enter Rudra's realm without the Grace of the Goddess

671. who knows that time is of the essence

672. who makes haste for she knows time is short and life is fleeting

673. who lives in the golden present

674. whose Samyama (one pointed focus upon her) a devotee obtains the entire inner universe through

675. who knows by overcoming sin a being ultimately wins

676. who has no judgment on sin, but knows it as a point of choice from which to learn and grow

677. who is simple elegance, yet elegantly simple

678. who is luxuriously simple and simply luxurious

679. who is Sadyojata Devi, the five-headed Shivani who protects the disciple in five directions

680. who understands Moses' wandering in the desert for forty years represents his spiritual Sadhana and practice that led to ascension

681. whose river of Shakti deep within represents the inner flowing land of milk and honey

682. who accepts all offerings both positive and negative as Maha Prasad, as supreme Divine blessings

683. who compassionately comes down into the valley of man rather than waiting for man to ascend to her mountain

684. who is a perfect celibate in thought, word, deed, and action

685. whose enlightenment is unending

686. whose ascension has no platform from which it was launched

687. whose Oneness has no beginning

688. who is the center of the hub of the revolving wheel

689. who appears to be still, but is indeed a top rapidly spinning

690. who supports the wisdom of the steady tortoise while she compassionately laughs at the impatient hare

691. who is the voice telling Rapunzel to let down her hair

692. who bridges the worship between the Buddhism of Mahayana and Hinayana

693. who is Arogya Mata, the mother who cures disease

OCEAN OF CONSCIOUSNESS

694. whose spontaneous Shakti balances Vata, Pitta, and Kapha doshas

695. whose breathes fire into those who have the disease of Vata

696. who cools the aggravation of the fires of Pitta by cooling the God Agni deep within the furnace of gastric digestion

697. who blows the Shakti of hot air and breath to dry out the inner derangement of moisture within Kapha Dosha

698. whose Shakti purifies when it slowly moves through Asti and Mamsa (bone and muscle) to fortify the body's frame and form

699. whose Shakti cleanses and sublimates the Shukra of Veerya and Raja Veerya, the power of sexual energy

700. whose transmitted Shakti enriches and balances Meda within the body to balance fat and weight

701. whose healing Shakti circulates and enlivens Rakta dhatu to remove the toxins of the blood

702. who concentrates her Shakti upon Meja or bone marrow to increase its meditative density and power

703. whose Shakti blends with Rasa to nourish the tissues to prevent aging and decay

704. who will bring the ancient splendor and glory of Africa into humanity's awareness in the new Golden Age

705. who laughs and giggles with the Serengeti hyenas on full moon nights

706. who is at play with the lion, baboon, and cheetah upon the African plains

73

707. who will reawaken the ancient wisdom of Ethiopia and other lands in this Golden Age

708. who works with little known African devas who long for the world to understand their native gifts and secrets

709. who bathes in the rhythm and flow of the music and song of the South African Spirit

710. who dances with rhythm and joy with African tribes of every land

711. who works to protect the mountain gorilla from the brutality of the ignorant

712. who cries when a baby chimp loses its mother to greed and theft

713. who will awaken the world to the lore, myth, and wisdom of African masters long buried and forgotten under the cruel desert sands

714. who is working with the compassionate to eradicate African poverty and disease upon this forgotten and forsaken land

715. who intimately channels and nurtures the Divine African feminine

716. who seeks to eradicate injustice for African women

717. who heals the African male from fear of female power

718. who is in awe and reverence of the bond of love, strength, and hope of the African mother for her innocent child

719. who knows the guarded secrets of the Shamans who covet and protect their knowledge within the jungles of the wild

720. who is the hope, spirit, and splendor within the voice of African song

721. whose vision and meditation engulf the African mountains like a cool mystical fog

722. who revels in the mighty cascade of waters within the valleys of the Nile

723. who lovingly brings the zebra, elephant, giraffe, and antelope to the water's edge, but never forces them to take a drink

724. who communes and converses with mountains like Kilamanjaro, Abu, Shasta, Meru, Annapoorna, and Himavan as if they were her own kith and kin

725. who is chakra vasini, the vaporous, sparkling essence that dwells, animates, and meanders in and through the 12 chakra spheres

726. who is Mohini, the fascinating and charming enchantress of illusion

727. who is Aishwarya Lakshmi, the most sensual and captivating form of fortune and riches

728. who is Avni Brahma, the beautiful Goddess united with Mother Earth that anchors our grounding and centeredness

729. who is Padmavati, the mistress of fortune and fame who silently walks upon water to manifest lotus blossoms under her feet

730. who is Surya Kumari, the Golden Goddess who emanates infinite rays from the sun's corona crown

731. who is Saubagya Lakshmi, the prosperous hand that blesses and bestows longevity and happiness in life and living

732. who is Shivani, the energy that energizes the right hemisphere of the brain

733. who is Brahmarandrini Kundalini, the shy and demure one passing through the top of the head and is thinner than the fiber of a lotus stalk

734. who is Yogeshwari initiating aspirants into the mysteries of yoga

735. who is Bhairavi or Tara, the warrior star whose terror we do not want to face when creating bad karma

736. who is Sivanandini, the bliss of pure Shiva or Unity Consciousness

737. who is Premamayi, the mother of love and compassion

738. who is Guru Ma Mayi, the mother in the form of the guru tatwa (principle)

739. who is Ananda Mayi Ma, the mother whose bliss is so expansive it is hard to bear within a physical form

740. who is Tejo Mayi, the mother of personified lights and hues

741. who is Shanti Mayi, the mother of peace and serenity

742. who is Rasasvini, the one that pervades the body to create perfect ecstasy and enthusiasm

743. who is Varahi, the boar-headed Goddess who removes negativity

744. who is Jagad Amba, the supreme mother of cosmology of the seen and unseen, and the known and unknown

745. who is Nata Rajini gracing the graceful with the talent of dance

746. who is Chinna Ma, the tiny midget Goddess who fools the foolish because her light body is omnipresent, omniscient, and omnipotent

747. who is held forever prisoner and captive by the insatiable desire to give Darshan to suffering humanity

748. whose form Avilokatewari sees as she reaches into the serene pond waters to caress the lilies

749. who is both Yin and Yang and yet neither Yang nor Yin

OCEAN OF CONSCIOUSNESS

750. who is at the center of the Dao

751. who sees the Devil or Mara as a child of the Divine

752. who guides and inspires the celestial physicians

753. who will forever be cherished by the Hawaiian Islands for gracing them with her living presence

754. who carries a goad to ensnare the negativity of ego

755. who holds a conch that reverberates the sound of Om

756. who lovingly adores and respects the shadowy night owl for its silent wisdom and wisdom in silence

757. who is Mira Shakti Devi, the ocean of consciousness who knows no separation between the foam and the wave or the depths of the sea

GLOSSARY

Missing lines or definitions have been intentionally left out because they have been explained or defined in the line and need no further explanation.

Line 5. Sankalpa is an act of will taken by a great master or teacher guru or divine mother. Through their will, linked directly with the Cosmic Source, the divine teacher or avatar can bring about changes in us and in the world in a much faster and expanded way. This is a great mystery we can know as we deepen our own consciousness within the mysteries of Source.

Line 9. Para Atma means the Supreme Divine Light or the Supreme Cosmic Soul.

Lines 1-10. Cosmic Source that is all pervasive decides to take on a body in various worlds and channel its Divine powers and qualities through a human being. It is the most direct way to reach humans limited in body and mind to help uplift and teach. The infinite Spirit has to come down to humans in a way they can relate. For those who recognize this, much benefit can be obtained from their direct guidance.

Definition: *Ganesh*: the elephant headed deity who represents obstacle removal for all and known in all cultures by various names and forms. He is the Divine form that helps us remove our inner and outer blocks to our own Divine and worldly path.

Line 17. *Soruba Samadhi*: this is a rare state of Oneness and Unity Consciousness that allows someone to be at one with the Divine and thus tap into any aspect and place in the Universe through his or her expanded consciousness.

Line 18. *Mahavatar Babaji* lives in the Himalayas for over 5,000 years, guiding humanity from the inner space of silence. Shirdi Sai Baba is a radiant being, who lived in the 19th century in Maharastria India, and performed endless miracles.

Line 20. *Kundalini Yoga*: the yoga of direct awakening of our dormant inner light and fire that exists within the spine. It ultimately travels to our head and breaks open the infinite Divine Source normally capped off from our conscious knowing.

Line 21. *Shambavi, Urvaretri, Urdvadristhti Siddha Yogini*: this is a Divine personality who has the ability to bear and allow the Divine kundalini to flow up to the brain and beyond. Its force is hard to bear. When this happens the eyes turn upward automatically and send light into the brain during Divine states of bliss and ecstasy roused in deep and arduous meditation over many lives.

Line 23. *Nirvikalpa Samadhi and Sahaja Avastha*: other Sankskit names that describe our ability to attain Unity Consciousness, where our mind merges with the Source so we do not experience separation between inner energy and us like an ocean drop merging into an ocean.

Definition. *Samadhi*: conscious union with the Divine; the human literally experiences expanded Unity Consciousness and no longer feels like a limited person.

Lines 26-32. These lines describe different actual states and visions we can have when we experience inner consciousness. Just as we gaze out to see beautiful scenery, there is beautiful scenery inside our own system when our gaze is turned inward in continuous meditation. Most of humanity is still unaware of this great but important mystery.

Definition. *Crown Chakra*: energy center at the top of the head. Seen in subtle shades of platinum, white, silver, gold periwinkle, rose, blue being, star, and pearl; distinct lights seen in advanced meditation states.

OCEAN OF CONSCIOUSNESS

Definition. *Visuddha Chakra*: the blue energy center located at the throat, which means space or ocean, and is an expressive expansion. Most often seen in shades of blue-green and teal color.

Definition. *Anahata and Hridaya*: energy centers surround and inside the chest or heart area. Anahata means sounds that arise without two items coming together to make a sound. Hridaya means that which contains Supreme compassion. Often visualized in hues of green.

Definition. *Solar Nadis*: the subtle nerve channels surrounding the solar plexii of nerves -- solar light body. The light body surrounding and within the physical body in which the solar plexus emanates powerful heat and light when awakened. Often seen in shades of yellow.

Definition. *Swadisthana "contemplation / flow of creativity:"* the center located in the genital region, which emanates creativity and sexual energy, intimacy, and expression. Often seen in shades of orange.

Definition. *Muladhar Chakra*: the red chakra at the base of the spine where kundalini energy lays dormant. Mula means root, where our sense of grounding and feeling of gravity and weight occurs for our anchoring onto the Earth. With grounding we can carry on earthly tasks in a clear and solid manner.

Line 49. *Darshan / Darshan Embrace*: Darshan means "to see" literally. It is a practice in the East for awakened teachers to see people individually in a process known as Darshan. Spending a few minutes or even seconds in close proximity to the aura and physical space of a guru, master, or a divine mother has a mysterious effect on each person. The sacred energy emanating around an enlightened person has the ability for others "to see" their own divinity that is buried by untold issues, blocks, or sufferings. By honoring a sacred person one-on-one, an individual honors him or herself because the two in that sacred moment of connection are mirroring divinity in each other. When kundalini energy rises and strikes the optic chiasm, the eyes for a period of time, on and off, are forced upward and gaze inward into the infinite space of the "akasha" or inner sky. This profound state comes and goes until one is fully established in the conscious experience of the inner sky and so the eyes return to normal. This kind of eyes upward vertical movement comes and goes for various periods of time and serves to create a completely solid, steady mind -- mind follows the eyes and vice versa. The life force flows through the eyes for our perception so the life force through the mind goes through the eyes.

Line 58. *Sadhana*: means spiritual practices of any kind that lead into expansion of consciousness through health, healing, medicine, and spirituality with a solid steady unwavering mind. Cosmic light can enter such a being so he or she can transmit this light to others. If the mind is choppy like a rough lake the light cannot clearly penetrate the mind to enter this world to others because the mind is not clear. It is like muddy murky water and cannot cleanly reflect light to others.

Definition. *Seva Vision*: expanded vision for selfless service to humanity for man kind's help and uplifting.

Line 68. *The dhatus*: there are subtle components of all the tissues in the body that carry energy -- in the bones, fat, blood, semen, etc.

Line 69. A guru or divine mother's spiritual power literally enters a seeker and begins to work on awakening the dormant forces within the human system.

Line 70. *Ayurveda*: the "Science of Life," which is the ancient system of medicine in East India.

Line 71. *Guru Sankalpa*: a guru's act of will that causes benefit to others through the literal transmission of energy to help heal or uplift.

Definition. *The Three Granthis*: there are three energy knots located at the base of the spine, the heart center, and the point between the two eyebrows. These energy knots tie our conscious tightly to the physical world and the body. A guru or Divine Mother has the ability to awaken an individual's kundalini and take that energy through the spine to piece these "knots," and in doing this karma is released and we can advance in our expansion of consciousness.

Line 72. *Ajna Chakra*: the center within the forehead -- the source of wisdom deep within our brain that carries energy.

Line 76. Beyond the primordial hum the highest consciousness is not explainable; it can only be experienced. The final experience is even beyond inner light and sound. We must pass through even the primordial hum's creative vibration to rest finally in the highest Source. A Divine Mother or highest enlightened teacher has this ability rediscovered through lifetimes of practice.

Lines 80-103. Dr. Rama was inspired from within to include a few names from the traditional 1000 names of the Divine Mother that were especially resonant with Mirabai. He was guided to select the names especially resonant with Mirabai. He was further inspired to write the translation and use the reference book *The Thousand Names Of The Divine Mother: Shri Lalita Sahasranama* written by Dr. M.N. Namboodiri.

Line 86. *Brahman*: a word for the absolute Source that is the primordial cause.

Lines 80-108. These lines are all attributes attained when an individual channels his or her Higher Self into a body and mind and offers these qualities to others for the uplifting of humanity.

Line 111. *The Four Kumaras*: these are the primordial "sons of the Source" personified as little kids -- four beings, Sanananda, Sanat Kumara, Sanatana, and Sanakya, who went through the universe to teach universal principles of truth and healing. The Cosmic Mother in the lore and literature of the ancients has a special fondness for the Kumaras, as they draw their energy from the Cosmic Feminine principle.

Line 114. *Yoga Maya*: the Divine Mother in her cosmic play creates the illusion of solidity in this physical world. In the duality of this universe, we think we are separated when in reality we are in Oneness. Without this separation "the show cannot go on." Yet, in this play, we have to play hide and seek with the Divine. In separation we are hiding from the Divine and in unity we find the Divine. Maya is the illusory power of the Divine Mother.

Line 115. *Gayatri "Gaia," Mother of the Earth, or Mother of All*: The aspect of the Divine in which the Vedas or sacred sounds and chants emanated from her Divine voice. She has multiple heads, which symbolize cosmic geometry, which make up all pervasive directions on this physical plane and other dimensions.

Line 116. *Kamakshi / Meenakshi*: embodiment of Love and alleviation of suffering; deities who increase love and relieve suffering.

Line 119. *The Great Sri Vidya Yantra*: this image contains sacred symbols and lines that represent the cosmos. At the center of this drawing is a red dot, which symbolizes the inner portal to cosmic consciousness that is seen in the center of the head in deep meditation. When it expands through the Grace of the Divine Mother once, it can literally expand and travel in the higher inner realms. These great mysteries are locked within the drawings and diagrams of ancient Hinduism.

Line 120. Shodashi is often depicted as a beautiful woman holding various objects that symbolize the unity of education, music, and power. Often in Hinduism, some goddesses' powers are fused into one "Super goddess."

Line 121. There is latent dormant spiritual power locked within the matrix of crystals yet to be harnessed by scientists and by those practicing inner spiritual pursuits.

Line 122. The Divine Mother essence flows through all cultures and bloodlines. Mirabai, in her previous lives, fused with the energy of the Cosmic Mother has worked with Western spiritual bloodlines and their ultimate destiny on this planet.

Line 130. *Chiti Shakti*: the power of the Divine Mother in the form of playful waves of light sent out through the primordial Source into manifested creation. These waves or particles of light dance and are responsible for the solidification and dissolution of atoms; this light also comprises the atoms -- all part of the dance of creation, preservation, and destruction. Chiti Shakti is honored in the East as the sacred nature of the Mother responsible for creation itself.

Line 131. *Kala Bhairava*: the aspect of Shiva or the Divine Source that is the Lord of Time. Bhairavi or Kali is the feminine Mistress of Time. The East honors the idea that time is our greatest friend and our greatest enemy and so we must always respect and honor time, which ultimately is also an illusion in the timeless cosmos.

Line 134. *Kali and Durga*: Divine Mother images, warrior goddesses. Kali is the controller and Mistress of Time. Durga means invincible.

Line 135. *Radha Bhav*: the Divine mood of Radha, the Mistress of Krishna, whose famous Love represents the union of the Divine Feminine and the Divine Masculine. Radha literally means "worship," derived from the root aradhana. The feminine principle "worships" the masculine krishna principle (the black primordial Source) in a play of cosmic dance and song.

Lines 157-160. Mirabai was guided to live upon the Hawaiian Islands to revel in their beauty and remember its land was once the ancient continent of Lemuria hundreds of thousands of years ago. Lemuria was a deeply spiritual culture where many are now incarnating into the modern world to bring back the remembrance of Spirit they learned when they were in this ancient culture from past lives.

Lines 161-165. A being like Mirabai uplifts and revels in all cultures. In her cosmic form, she has worked from time immemorial to uplift various cultural lineages of this planet and many other countless worlds.

Lines 165. Destiny landed Mirabai's birth in Africa and was much needed to remove many ancient curses and difficulties in that land. Africa is the gateway of East and West and so in this incarnation her form took birth in that land.

Line 169. *The Ancient Minotaur*: the ancient Greek entity half human and half bull. Heroes led themselves out of captivity out of the labyrinth from imprisonment by the king. If they did not get out, this beast would eat them. The labyrinth represents our own chaotic and dissipated mind that we have to walk through to get into a state of enlightenment or be devoured by our negative ego.

Line 170. *Sattva / Gunas*: there are three main qualities of mind: sattva, rajas, and gunas -- the tranquil, dull, and active parts of mind. Sattva is the tranquil part of mind that a Divine Mother acts through to uplift the spiritual parts of our being.

Line 172. The guru's sandals represent the right and left-brain lobes that look like two sandals sitting in our head. Worshipping the sandals represent awakening our brain into greater expanded consciousness. Outer worship of actual sandals connects us to the awakening of the inner brain in a very deep and mysterious process known in the East as the "Guru-disciple" relationship.

Line 190. *108*: a sacred number that reduces to the number three, and is poetic and symbolic of her in this line.

Line 198. Vayu (wind element), Agni (fire element), Bhoomi (earth element), Jala (water element), and Akasha (ethereal or cosmic space element).

Line 201. *The New Golden Age*: began in 2012, and will continue for 10,200 years on this planet and in this solar system, as this system passes through the photon belt surrounding the Pleiades Star System. The physical passing of light over the next 10,200 years will affect the physical system and the subtle light will affect our inner subtle system, causing an expansion of enlightenment so this planet and other worlds will evolve into higher thinking, life, and living.

Line 208. *Vak Nadi*: Vak is a name of Saraswati, whose energy is located at the tip of the tongue. A subtle nerve channel flows from the tip of the tongue all the way past the inner heart. When awakened the power of creativity, oration, elocution, and wisdom are activated fully, long forgotten in the human experience.

Line 221. *Rama and Sita*: incarnations of the Divine, who also held Twin Flame love; their story is in the Ramayana (the story of Rama).

OCEAN OF CONSCIOUSNESS

Line 223. *Lalithananda*: the blissful play of benevolence, welcoming, charm, and Grace, a key aspect of the Divine Mother, known as Lalitha Devi -- the root lalitha means spontaneous and easy. This form of mother is easy to approach for she is gentle and kind, and communicative in nature.

Line 225. *Akasha Records*: in the ethers there exist karma records of everyone and everything. An individual can attain the power to focus and read his/her own past karma and those of others. A Divine Mother being can easily access these records to understand a person and help them on their path by knowing their past, present, and future.

Line 230. *Shrotiya*: one who perfects worldly and spiritual skills.

Line 238. *Uma Devi*: the Divine Mother in the form of pure beauty; the root means tranquility, splendor, fame, and "night." The goddess is often depicted with a dark complexion.

Line 249. *Kriyavati*: subtle and physical movements, releases, or changes that sometimes manifest as bodily movements or other sudden mental thoughts or emotions. After receiving a kundalini awakening, "kriyas" constantly occur on any and all levels, sometimes in our awareness to purify and expel any and all negativity that keeps the flow of kundalini from moving freely and permanently within our system. This is a great and mysterious science few in this world still have the skill to master and truly teach.

Line 253. *Istha Devata*: image of the Divine that sometimes takes a form within the mind to help uplift, communicate, and teach us what we need to know. Personified being that symbolizes our own inner knowing and guidance.

Line 254. *Prarabdha, Sanchita and Agami Karma*: these are the energy thought impressions we create from countless lives within us that preceded this birth, energies within this birth being burned up and exhausted, and future impressions that will bear fruit in future births. A true guru or Divine Mother has the power to burn up these karmas and fry them literally so these karma seeds or impressions cannot germinate into future births.

Line 261. *Vajreshwari*: the Goddess in the form of thunder and sound, often worshipped in South India.

Line 262. At one stage of meditation, an individual passes through dark murmuring clouds. This is also known as Mother Kali, one of the Divine moods of the Goddess Kundalini. When she travels through our system, we experience any and all images and moods of the Goddess. Passing through these clouds, an individual is left with an awe inspiring, eerie feelings, because the clouds seem endless.

Line 264. *Aurora Rani (the Queen of Light or Ojas Shakti)*: our inner luster generated from our own unique life force that percolates through our body and mind; unique for each person with no two forms of Ojas ever alike.

Line 265. Recognized in Ayurveda Medicine, Mej is fatty marrow that contains rich nutrients. When kundalini is awakened, she feeds off of this energy to fuel and increase her power within the body and mind. These subtle principles are virtually unknown in Western Medicine.

Line 272. *Apana Shakti*: there are five different basic flows in our system that the life force rides upon. Apana shakti causes our system to flow downward, such as the process of orgasm, urination, menstruation, defecation, and childbirth. Without apana these downward processes are not possible. The Divine Mother is honored because she is this apana or energy that flows in different directions in the body. Worship, chanting and other spiritual practices corrects the flow in our system, which is blocked by various diseases on all levels so we cannot experience optimal health and healing.

Line 275. Souls who take birth begin to awaken and realize they are trapped again into a womb and the cycle of birth and death after being free in the Heavens for a period of time. The Divine Mother has compassion for these beings who must endure cosmic law by once again becoming ensnared into a body through their own choosing, desires, and karma. The soul knows it is going to be limited again and cries out to the Divine Mother for release; however, they must remain due to their own karma for positive and negative learning in this kind of physical world.

Line 277. *Ida and Pingala Nadis*: two nerve channels alongside the central spinal column. The two together are symbolized in the caduceus. When completely pure, Kundalini can flow unending and through these channels to create the fulfilled human, but are still rarely seen on this planet due to lack of understanding and practice. Ida and Pingala represent male and female principles or sun and moon. When awakened and flowing, we experience the perfect balance of androgyny.

Line 305. In the Bhagavad Gita, the character was alongside Krishna on a battlefield. Remorseful of upcoming killings of his relatives, Arjuna was shirking his warrior duties. Krishna on the battlefield reassured him of his righteous role or sacred duty. Then, he touched him and bestowed the experience of Cosmic Consciousness, where Arjuna saw simultaneously the entire inner cosmos at any and all levels. He could not bear the intensity for very long. However, a Divine Mother being has the power to bear this continuously for the sake of humanity as an Avatar, and this is still not seen very much on this planet just yet. Swaroopa means the infinite consciousness within one's own inner being.

Lines 314-315. *Shabda and Various Sounds*: these cosmic sounds are heard in deep meditation and upon passing away at death. When we listen to the highest sounds they act as a road map for the soul to go to higher realms by following the sounds as an actual travel path. The soul finally bypasses all dimensions that correspond to different sounds heard to rest in the soundless Source. This can happen while living in a body or after passing away at physical death. Depending on our skill and awakening, we pick the highest level we can handle and go on to rest and learn while living or dead.

Line 334. *Siddhis*: Divine latent powers of all kinds most humans at their present stage of evolution have not used or awakened. However, enlightened masters have various awakenings and talents unknown to mankind.

Lines 336-359. These lines are a poetic description of Mirabai's biography and her early path to the Divine.

Line 363. The Star of David literally exists in the form of Light within the crown chakra and can be seen in deep meditation.

Definition. *Sahasrar*: a thousand petaled lotus of light that is sitting in, through, and above the brain in various degrees of awakening in all people.

Line 364. The Star of the East is literally a Divine star of light located between the pineal and pituitary gland. The three wise men saw this in their inner meditation. It was not an outer star in the sky. They received Divine guidance to visit Jesus through telepathy from guides, who use the spiritual star or eye as a vehicle of psychic communication.

Line 365. The Divine Mother beings automatically can read any phase of Earth's or any planetary history. In the 21st century or so it will be revealed that Jesus lived in India and that his missing 33 years were spent in the Himalayas.

Line 366. Atlantis and Lemuria are two of many ancient advanced cultures on Earth. Scientists are revealing Earth had advanced civilizations that have come and gone over 20 million years or more.

Line 367. Like many planets and civilizations, cultures perished when they placed technology over spirituality rather than respecting both equally. This happened to Atlantis and can happen to us also if we do not understand deeper spirituality, along with technology.

Line 370. *Samskaras*: mental and emotional impressions based in our desires and experiences. Our impressions create samskaras and then karma, which remain deep within our unconscious, subconscious, pre-conscious, and conscious minds. These impressions are the root cause of taking birth in this and countless other worlds for endless periods of times, until a full inner enlightenment burns away these seeds so we no longer are bound by cosmic law to take birth in this realm.

Line 372. *The Great Void (Maha Shunya or the Fourth World):* The eerie blackness seen in meditation that is seemingly endless and infinite. It exists between above the throat and below the point of the eyebrows. There is also another void between the eyebrows and the crown of the head. Our souls must cross this void to enter the sphere of unmanifest light located in the crown for permanent enlightenment to occur. This is only possible through the Grace of enlightened masters in this world and beyond.

Line 403. *Gaia*: another word for Mother Earth, as previously explained.

Line 422. The different Lakshmis or divine Mothers of Abundance represent different forms of abundance: courage, money, power, prestige, inner and outer beauty, higher Self-qualities, successful childbirth, and countless other forms.

Line 423. Sundara Lakshmi traditionally has an extra toe representing her sovereign nature as the highest form of Motherly Abundance.

Line 430. *White Buffalo Calf*: a sacred form of the Divine Mother, who takes birth as a white calf. Very rare and auspicious, several have been mercilessly slaughtered in recent times. The white calf symbolizes the dawn of the Golden Age foreseen by ancient Native Americans.

Line 431. The Islamic world, through their culture, chooses to veil Divine femininity behind cloak and veil. One day this power in that world will be fully understood.

Line 434. These words (Jivan Mukta, Siddha, Avadoota, and Arhat) are describing various levels of enlightened beings; they each have their talents and abilities in these various states of consciousness.

Line 452. Traditionally there are 27 different levels and types of intensities of Kundalini awakening, of which a Divine Mother being has mastered and knows what and how much to give to others.

Line 455. Countless souls wait for eons for birth into a situation that will foster spiritual growth. These souls wait for the birth of a Divine Guru or Divine Mother to learn from them. Not all planets are graced with this spirituality, as many planets are focused more on materialism and technology. So, many wait and wait and are finally granted the grace of an actual physical teacher, who helps them on their journey to enlightenment. The highest enlightenment still often needs some kind of physical world and body to liberate on into higher worlds for further learning and service. Again, these are deep and great mysteries that take volumes to learn and explain.

Lines 464-466. In one system of classification there are five bodies including the physical, one inside the other. When kundalini is activated we begin to have awareness of these bodies at different times. When completely awakened we truly becomes super human beings in flesh form -- a Divine personality while living in a body.

Lines 470-476. These are mystery goddesses seen within the chakras as the Kundalini energy pierces these areas. They offer blessings and powers to those who see them in these deeply meditative states. Our solar system's planets influence each of these goddesses and powers. This is a very deep science that has to be studied deeply in mystery schools when we are ready.

Line 477. When kundalini hits various nerve centers these sounds described are heard. They indicate many different angles and facets of knowledge. Hearing them once is ever increasingly expanded on the road to the mysteries of inner enlightenment.

Line 478. The salt doll is the symbolic image of humans and their limited thinking and minds. When real enlightenment occurs, the small Self merges into the inner Great Self and so there is no longer the feeling of separation from the Divine.

Line 495. The 8th chakra above the crown is the gateway to even higher levels of awareness and consciousness, which are hard to bear while in a human body. A Divine Mother has all 12 chakras awakened (five more above the crown). There is no way to describe these infinite states; they must be experienced. Most humans in their present state of evolution are completely unaware of these matters.

Line 497. The Cosmic Source speaks in one way through our right ear if we tune in to hear, but can guide us in any manner through our knowing and senses anyway.

Line 498. When the inner crown chakra is awakened the pituitary gland releases ambrosial nectar, which is cosmic energy that travels downward onto the tongue and the rest of the body. We experience continuous rejuvenation so fatigue, the need for sleep, food, sex, and water, etc. are eventually transcended.

Line 499. *Hemagiri Nandini*: a very deeply symbolic form of Parvati or Divine Mother, who lived in the Himalayas ages ago and merged with Shiva her divine ascetic consort. This union symbolizes the ascent of kundalini up the mountain into the crown for complete union of Divine male and female principles. Hemagiri means the one of red luster. Kundalini is often seen as a red line through the body. Nandini is the female energy that surrounds the Divine cow Nandi, who represents the sacred white bull in our throat. Through Nandi we ascend via the head into the realm of Shiva. This symbology is very deep. There are countless physical images of these deities in India that represent deep inner meditative processes.

Line 517. A great master or Mother often gestures gracefully when receiving people one-by-one. This is the dance of kundalini sending messages through the teacher's body as symbolic meaning for each person, and is unique for each as these teachers receive him or her in a greeting line after meditations and programs.

Line 524. *Merkabah*: one type of inner vehicle the soul literally rides to travel to inner worlds. It is not the highest vehicle, however. There are many others unknown to mankind and must be experienced through meditation and spiritual practice.

Line 525. The Solar Dynasties are the beings located in the great area of our central galaxy. There are countless enlightened beings in the center who sometimes come to this Earth plane that teach mankind.

Line 528. There is nothing the Divine cannot do or hear simultaneously at all times without end or break. This is a concept is one of many our limited mind cannot grasp fully.

Line 534. The Divine knowing is beyond the senses. A fully enlightened individual does not need to depend on the limited senses to gather knowledge for they have tapped into the cosmic Source for these purposes.

Line 535. The inner sounds do not need objects to strike to hear, and are known as the sound of one hand clapping. These sounds are causeless and spontaneous and arise out of the bliss of the Creator.

Line 536. The tree of life is upside down, which means cosmic energy descends through our body to awaken our kundalini so our consciousness once again ascends. The imagery is part of the flow of sap in a tree. It is depicted upside down because energy has to descend before the sap can ascend from the roots.

Line 540. There are countless animal deities and half human half animal archetypes that are real and exist. They all honor the Divine Mother beings and vice versa.

Line 558. The Hawaiian Islands, particularly the island of Kauai, have higher awakenings. The subtle higher dimensions are often far away from the Earth plane's reach. However, in Kauai the dimensions are very close between physical and subtle, and so holy and sacred energy flows more easily in that world. The rest of the world has to catch up in varying degrees.

Line 564. Many defects and tears exist in our subtle bodies, which bring disease. A Divine Mother or Guru knows how to repair these.

Line 565. Continuation: and knows how to awaken and develop the light body and other subtle bodies.

Line 566. Jesus taught enlightenment methods he also shared and learned in India. Today's churches are not aware of kundalini awakening and methods of Yoga. Jesus himself taught and so these methods remain only at a certain level of understanding that will change in this Golden Age.

Line 583. *Pranam*: respectful salutations.

OCEAN OF CONSCIOUSNESS

Line 589. Enlightenment is already present. There is nothing to attain ultimately. It is only a matter of remembering what is already present inside us.

Lines 593-598. These lines represent the yoga and practice of wisdom, devotion, selfless service, meditation, repetition of sacred names, and physical postures.

Line 611. Deep within the crown, within the Star of David, sounds "A KA Tha" can be heard. These thrilling sounds force the soul into the higher states of the crown center and above, just like rocket fuel blasts a rocket off. We are left with intense bliss and joy when we come back down into ordinary consciousness.

Line 612. Previously explained.

Line 613. This line describes the actual exploding of the Little Blue Pearl. The Great Soul is a great mystery. When it permanently explodes, we are left in a state of very high enlightenment. However, it does not end there. Consciousness goes on in an unending unfolding of states of being even beyond the Blue Pearl explosion.

Line 614. The Non-regressing Bodhi Sattva is recognized in Buddhist literature. This is where we are enlightened and cannot go back into the trap of lower delusional qualities of the lower mind. We are at a point of no return of inner purity and can only go upward. It is a critical stage of development that a Divine Mother graces for their upward and onward expansion of consciousness and Higher Self qualities.

Line 616. In ordinary states of consciousness, burdened by karma, we sometimes cannot bear the purity of such an enlightened soul. We sometimes run away, attack or criticize, and misunderstand these enlightened beings' intentions and missions.

Line 617. The Divine Mother exists at all times and in all spaces. It was her Divine force that inspired Harriet Tubman to use the secrets of moss to free slaves.

Line 620. *The Middle Path*: the balanced path of not too much or too little of anything to attain enlightenment rediscovered by the Buddha after he went to extremes in the name of spiritual practice unnecessarily.

Line 621. Taking on a body is painful for unlimited Cosmic Mothers and Masters who feel the body weighs them down and, yet they must have one to directly communicate with the physical world. Others communicate without the body, but most people are not awake enough to fully receive their guidance. This is why enlightened Mothers and Masters have to come down in bodily form.

Line 624. In cosmic consciousness Divine Mothers feel the pains, joys, and sorrows of sentient and insentient beings because they are merged in Unity consciousness. Everything others feel, they feel in their own bodies and minds.

Line 637. *Savikalpa Samadhi*: a state of consciousness that requires motionlessness of the body. It evolves into Nirvikalpa Samadhi or Sahaja Avastha, which means Unity consciousness that can be handled at all times and does not need bodily stillness. Savikalpa is still limited. This line describes the freedom of Nirvikalpa Samadhi like taking off in a hot air balloon for more mental freedom.

Line 640. The sun sends out burning rays in all directions but is untouched by the heat; similarly, a Divine Mother sends out this heat and light but is not affected because she is heat and light.

Line 642. The Holy Grail drink is the actual inner ambrosia generated from the pituitary. When this nectar descends through the system, we feel eternally youthful and attain immortality. It has been misinterpreted to be an outer object. A Divine Mother like Mirabai has this nectar flowing at all times.

Line 645. Inner power is latent in most humans; we are using only a fraction of our inner power. Just as fire is latent in wood, a Divine Mother awakens its heat and power inside our dormant being.

Line 649. There are some ET races that are not so nice!! The Divine Mother still sends unconditional love as part of the respect for positive and negative as she exists within and transcends both.

OCEAN OF CONSCIOUSNESS

Line 650. A symbolic metaphor, sacred yagna fires are ancient Hindu fires performed today that invoke various forms of spiritual power.

Line 655. Somayaji is an exact science. Through external fire ritual and chanting, spiritual energy can manifest and uplift those who attend. Similarly, there is the inner fire where inside of us. Divine heat also creates Soma or again Divine nectar that bathes the cells and rejuvenates body and mind.

Line 659. From the Bible dying daily means to enter cosmic unity consciousness when the mind and body are stilled. At the time of real death there is no fear because we are used to going in and out of the body anyway in states of meditation, only to come back into ordinary life.

Line 660. Each Master or Divine Mother brings in their own unique energy, spirit, gifts, talents, and abilities and so they are all honored as unique and worthy.

Lines 664-668. The kundalini pierces all of the described knots so we gradually realize simultaneous expanded states of awareness while in a body. This is what being multidimensional means. We become aware of ourselves at all levels at once, something a Divine Mother being automatically does.

Line 669. Already explained. The Nandi cow, the Divine vehicle or Modaka of Shiva, represents the throat center. In Hindu temples there is always the statue of Nandi sitting in front of the image of Shiva to symbolize the Kundalini has to pass through the throat to reach the crown to which Shiva's consciousness is located.

Line 678. *Sadyojata*: five headed beings representing five major directions. It also represents the five areas of the brain awakened when the secret Kundalini passes through the brain: Parietal, Cortex, Frontal, Occipital, and Temporal lobes. Often seen on images of male and female deities.

Line 690. "Letting down one's hair" means being vulnerable in the heart to feelings, emotions, and new experiences.

Line 691. Mahayana and Hinayana: the great paths of Buddhism that reflect the formless path to the Divine and the one that involves form.

Lines 692-702. This section describes a Divine Mother like Mirabai, who can work with the actual bodily tissues and life force behind each tissue. What is written is only a tiny fraction of this knowledge. The Vata Pitta and Kapha Doshas refer to our bodily constitution based in the five elements of air, water, fire, and ether. The Kundalini energy transmitted from Mother to us has the ability to shape shift its form and qualities to cure us of our ailments. It thus becomes cool, hot, warm, fluid, or solid and so on based on our unique problems. The energy transmitted has its own intelligence. It knows what to do, where to go, and what to work on for us once transmitted from the Divine through that Divine Mother to us. This section is giving a tiny sample of what this energy can do along with the actual physical science of medicine known as Ayurveda. It is rare to have someone enliven the body along with the gross physical practices and prescriptions given with the Ayurvedic treatment. That is why this planet is awakening back to long lost ancient secrets that combine energy transmission with physical healing.

Lines 705-722. This is a delightful set of lines that came through to celebrate Mirabai's birth upon the sacred but troubled land of Africa. She dances with Nature and Nature dances with her.

Lines 725-747. These are celebrations of interesting and inspiring Vedic names of the goddess already described in the line.

Line 724. *Chakra Vasini*: the sacred Goddess essence that dwells and animates the life force and body. Chakra vasini is the Goddess herself who animates the subtle and gross elements of body and mind. Without this animation, the body and mind are useless and lifeless. Vasini also means the one who creates impressions or vasanas.

Line 725. *Mohini*: the fascinatingly beautiful form of Narayana the Pervasive Male Lord of the Created Worlds. Mohini is the Goddess who captivates through illusion and is another form of Maya. Maya manifests to trick the negative ego or demons into thinking the created world is real when in reality it is an illusory play of light, shadow, and sound suffused with primordial Love. Only in realizing and experiencing primordial Love inside the heart that has no cause can we understand the nature of how unreal the outer world really is.

Line 731. *Shivani*: the feminine form of Shiva; her energy is concentrated in the right brain and left side of the body's Ida nerve channel, while Shiva is the male energy mainly situated in the left brain that affects the right side of the body's Pingala nerve channel. It proves true in modern medicine where the right brain involves emotions, intuition, and feelings, while the left brain is more doing, thinking, processing, and analyzing (i.e., female and male issues, respectively).

Line 748. The ultimate Divine is beyond male and female principles (i.e., Yin and Yang) and yet, pervades both. Hard to explain and comprehend but in a Divine Mother's enlightenment and in our own we realize we, too, are beyond and yet within the male and female energies.

Line 749. The center of the Dao is the bindu -- the tiny soul. Deep inside us, when it explodes, we experience complete Oneness with the Source. A Divine Mother exists at the center of this mysterious dot. What seems tiny can expand to embrace the entire cosmos.

ABOUT THE AUTHOR

Rama Pemmaraju Rao is a physician, who enjoys writing on health, healing, spirituality, creativity, and medicine. He is inspired to write children's stories that offer lessons and meaning. His lifelong journey and work is to honor the body, awaken the mind, and expand the heart to rediscover the spirit within. Visit his website at DrRamaEnlightenmentMD.com.

OTHER BOOKS BY RAMA PEMMARAJU RAO

Be "SELF"-Centered (not self-centered)
Expanding and enlightening our small self to
unite with the Divine SELF or Source

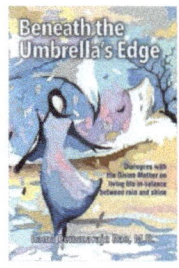

Beneath the Umbrella's Edge
Dialogues with the Divine Mother on living life
in balance between rain and shine

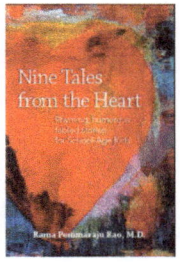

Nine Tales from the Heart
Rhyming, humorous fabled stories for School-Age Kids

Raindrops Upon the Parched Fields of My Heart
Soul Wisdom for the Awakening Heart

These books are available at authorhouse.com,
barnesandnoble.com, and amazon.com.

For further information and inspiration visit Dr. Rama's new works in progress on his website at www.drramaenlightenmentmd.com

ABOUT THE PAINTINGS – FRONT AND BACK COVER ART

Front and back cover art by Rama Pemmaraju Rao, MD. Front cover: *Mirabai Immersed in Divine Light*. Back cover: *Mirabai Enthroned Upon the Altar of Eternity and Oneness*. Paintings by Dr. Rama Pemmaraju Rao directly reflect his soul inspiring energy that manifests images of health, healing, spirituality, creativity, and medicine through the mediums of oils, charcoal, and pencil. He captures the beauty of spirit's kaleidoscope of image and form. He looks forward to a cornucopia of artwork through his own renaissance of the heart that has been awakening and unfolding throughout his entire lifetime, especially since 2012.

ACKNOWLEDGEMENTS

Many thanks to the Divine Light, to Mirabai Devi, and all of the other masters, mentors, gurus, avatars, divine mothers, savants, sages, rishis, teachers, light beings, friends, and all others who have been supportive of me over many years in my own journey to the Self and my progression to an ever deepening enlightenment I am learning really has no end.

Much gratitude and the appreciation for the beings of light, guides, and guidance who gifted Mirabai with this book using me as an instrument based on ancient soul contracts I have shared with her in eternity.

May all enjoy reading this sacred text and contemplating its deep and profound meaning, and in doing so, come to realize that we, too, are none other than the Divine Love and Light expounded in these 756 poetic lines.

Deep appreciation for the main editor Sherwood Lee for her painstaking but rewarding efforts at editing, formatting, and commenting on this complex yet inspiring work as she "rescued" this project to bring into the Light for all. Also, my deep appreciation to Pat Dunlap at Dixie Studios for her all-around support and steadfastness on this project and to the beautiful website she works so diligently on that will one day cradle this amazing work of art and dedication, and many of my future creative endeavors.

Rama Pemmaraju Rao, MD
Spring 2016

Mirabai Devi is a deep and profound teacher, who is an embodiment of the Divine Mother. She holds various healing and enlightening aspects of the infinite cosmic feminine principle to bring her power, talents, and gifts to global humanity. She is one of the original female mentors and guides of Dr. Rama Pemmaraju Rao, who in working with her for a time, has been inspired to channel these 756 names, attributes, qualities, and descriptions about her Higher Self-essence.

Everyone in human form has various interesting personality twists and turns with unique issues; India still honors these beings because they channel a high energy of love and light for the benefit of humanity.

No one, including great teachers, enter this physical world or similar realm on other planets and worlds, including Mirabai, without their own valuable private lessons to learn, both positive and negative. They are still human beings relating and living in a human world with all of its fascinating flaws and imperfections mixed with joys and gifts. Jesus and any and all other spiritually historic Masters and Divine Mothers all had unique gifts to bring to humanity and struggled with their own inner trials and tribulations to understand and grow from.

This is the fascinating dance of enlightenment within a human body and life, enjoying the bliss of Higher Self and, yet still having to understand the limitations and woes of human life and living made clear, just as Jesus reminded us of the issues of the "Son of Man" vs. the "Son of God" (i.e., the play between his human life as a man and the Divinity he also carried for global uplifting). This inner and outer journey of understanding is thus the same with all great teachers from all traditions.

Yet, still, India has a tradition that when a sacred and spiritual being comes to this planet, 108 names are channeled and written down to describe such an individual and is passed onto generations for that teacher's remembrance and honor. Yet, in this instance, 756 lines have been created as a gift to her and to humanity from her guides within the Divine Light, and yet to come are 108 times five more for the other five spiritual centers that are rarely known.

In this fascinating book of 756 lines (108 lines for each of our 7 energy centers), Dr. Rama eloquently writes in a unique form of fused poetry/prose about profound areas of truth, healing, awakening, and enlightenment Mirabai and other Divine Mothers throughout the centuries harness into their own system to serve as instruments to send their love, blessings, spiritual power, and Grace to help uplift humanity on all levels. It is all a sacred and deep process where there is no beginning and no end to understanding the greatest mysteries of Spirit and Source.

Enjoy this powerful work that ultimately brings about our own remembrance of our Higher Self. Although tailored by her Heavenly guides to describe her and her mission, these descriptions also pave the way to remember each and every one of us is also the essence of the Divine Feminine and the Sacred Masculine. Yet, our ultimate enlightened essences are beyond both, as we realize we are ourselves the Divine Source. Reading or chanting these lines out loud brings about an instantaneous sense of joy, wonder, astonishment, love, and light as these lines are suffused with the blessings of high guides and guidance for the benefit of all. These lines indeed create an energy link to Universal Devine Feminine, which is none other than an integral facet of our own higher self.

www.ingramcontent.com/pod-product-compliance
Lightning Source LLC
Chambersburg PA
CBHW060925170426
43192CB00024B/2897